Concordia Parish Library

I0632961

FERRIDAY

OCT 9 2017

COPY 1

240 WAH
Wahlen, Clinton.
Women's ordination : does
it matter?

NO LONGER THE PROPERTY OF
CONCORDIA PARISH LIBRARY

FERRIDAY

Concordia Parish Library
Ferriday, Louisiana

WOMEN'S
ORDINATION
Does It Matter?

CLI

Cover design by Haley Trimmer
Interior design by Ken McFarland
Copyright © 2015 by Clinton and Gina Wahlen
Printed in the United States of America
All Rights Reserved

Bright Shores Publishing
P. O. Box 4826
Silver Spring, MD 20914
www.womensordination.com

Except where otherwise noted, Scripture quotations are from the New King James Version® (NKJV). Copyright © 1982 by Thomas Nelson, Inc. Used by permission. All rights reserved. All italics appearing in Scripture quotations are added for emphasis.

Scripture quotations marked ESV are taken from the ESV® Bible (The Holy Bible, English Standard Version®), copyright © 2001 by Crossway, a publishing ministry of Good News Publishers. Used by permission. All rights reserved.

Scripture quotations marked KJV are taken from the King James Version, public domain.

Scripture quotations marked NASB or NAS95 are taken from the New American Standard Bible®, copyright © 1960, 1962, 1963, 1968, 1971, 1972, 1973, 1975, 1977, 1995 by The Lockman Foundation. Used by permission. (www.Lockman.org.)

Scripture quotations marked NIV or NIV11 are from THE HOLY BIBLE, NEW INTERNATIONAL VERSION®, NIV® Copyright © 1973, 1978, 1984, 2011 by Biblica, Inc.™ Used by permission. All rights reserved worldwide.

Scripture quotations marked NRSV are taken from the New Revised Standard Version Bible, copyright © 1989 National Council of the Churches of Christ in the United States of America. Used by permission. All rights reserved.

ISBN: 978-0-9962661-0-9

COPY 1

CONTENTS

Concordia Parish Library
Ferriday, Louisiana

DEDICATION

To our daughter

Heather Grace Wahlen

and

all young women

whose heart's desire is to serve the Lord

ACKNOWLEDGMENTS

This book represents the work of many minds, and grows out of many ideas and suggestions from members of the General Conference Theology of Ordination Study Committee (GC-TOSC), as well as countless interactions with colleagues and friends, including cordial discussions with members of the North American Division Theology of Ordination Study Committee (NAD-TOSC) and division Biblical Research Committees worldwide. A number of Bible scholars, teachers, pastors, and lay people have carefully read and contributed to this book.

We would especially like to thank Dr. George Reid, former Director of the Biblical Research Institute (BRI) and Dr. Gerhard Pfandl, long-time Associate Director of the Biblical Research Institute for their reading and endorsing of this book.

We are also grateful to Dr. Ingo Sorke, Professor of Religion at Southwestern Adventist University in Keene, Texas, for taking time from his busy teaching schedule to review the manuscript and write an endorsement.

We are grateful to Shelley J. Quinn, Speaker and Co-Director for *Word Warrior Ministries.* In spite of a packed schedule, Shelley carefully read the manuscript and wrote an endorsement. As a best-selling Christian author and popular Bible teacher, Shelley Quinn travels extensively in the United States and internationally, preaching the Gospel of Christ at revivals, retreats, and camp meetings. She works in program development at *Three Angels Broadcasting Network* and hosts *Exalting His Word* and many other programs seen around the world on 3ABN.

We want to thank Sikhu Hlatshwayo for her incisive comments and endorsement. Sikhu is a graduate of Wellesley College in Massachusetts, has served as a campus chaplain, and is currently the Administrator for the Center of Adventist Ministry to Public University Students (CAMPUS), in East Lansing, Michigan.

An especially big thank you goes to our daughter, Heather Grace Wahlen, for meticulously going through the manuscript, asking helpful questions, checking readability, and for her proofreading accuracy. Heather Grace is currently studying at Fountainview Academy, in British Columbia, Canada, where she enjoys playing the piano and French horn with the internationally recognized and televised Fountainview Academy Orchestra and Singers.

We deeply appreciate the many friends who have supported this book project with their encouragement, prayers, godly counsel, practical wisdom, and timely advice.

Finally, we would like to thank you, the reader, for taking the time to carefully and prayerfully consider what is presented in this book. We are grateful to God for granting us the privilege of writing it, and our sincere prayer is that you will find this material to be a blessing as you seek for clarity on the important issues presented here.

WHAT READERS ARE SAYING...

From: George Reid, Ph.D.

Director of the Biblical Research Institute (retired)

With this volume you have an unusual discussion by an internationally recognized New Testament scholar— Dr. Clinton Wahlen—and his wife Gina, who is gifted with special writing skills. Together, they bring to readers a discussion of the ordination question both loyal to the biblical content and in readable language that opens it to everyone. With his doctorate from England's prestigious Cambridge University, he has taught in universities in several countries. Currently he is an associate director of the Biblical Research Institute in North America. Thank you for the major contribution this book makes to the biblical foundation of God's expressed will.

From: Gerhard Pfandl, Ph.D.

Associate Director of the Biblical Research Institute (retired)

The question of women's ordination has become a major issue in the Seventh-day Adventist Church. Contrary to the idea that the Bible does not address this issue, the Bible has much to say concerning the role of women in the Church. The authors of this book clearly demonstrate that we are not left without divine guidance on this issue. Not only are difficult Bible texts interpreted in harmony with the historical-biblical method, Ellen White's nuanced statements on the role of women are clearly presented. In addition the book addresses the question of what roles and positions women should occupy in the Church without changing the God-appointed structure of ministries in the Church.

In order to support the ordination of women in the Church, a new method of interpretation has been introduced. With the help of the "Principle-based Reading" method, which emphasizes that Scripture is culturally conditioned, all the texts that speak against the ordination of women are reinterpreted and explained away. If we as a Church ever accept this method, we will no longer be able to defend a six-day Creation or our position on homosexuality. Therefore, the book *Women's Ordination: Does It Matter?* is a must read for all members of the Seventh-day Adventist Church. Not only because of the divisive issue of women's ordination, but because acceptance of the "Principle-based Reading" method will impact our positions on a number of important teachings forever.

From: Ingo Sorke, Ph.D.

Professor of Religion, Southwestern Adventist University

In a sea of conflicting opinions and voices on women's ordination, Clinton and Gina Wahlen have produced a book of refreshing clarity, fairness, and simplicity. It is biblical, honest, and offers a welcome combination of readability and scholarly finesse. The book adequately addresses all major areas of concern concisely *and* comprehensively: the issues at stake, the biblical data, historical perspectives, gender roles, women in ministry (extensive research!), and practical implications for the Church. Lay persons, administrators, and scholars alike will find in this brief volume accessible answers to the most commonly posed questions. The Question and Answer section is especially helpful for quick reference, along with informative Appendices. *Women's Ordination— Does it Matter?* deserves to be read by the Church at such a time as this. No matter which side of the issue you find yourself on, this study deserves our attention—not the least for the unique fact that it was written by a husband-wife team. Timely wisdom for a Church at the crossroads! *Women's Ordination: Does It Matter?* was written for such a time as this. Highly recommended!

From: Shelley Quinn

Author and 3ABN Program Development Manager

With cultural tensions on the rise, there is an urgent need for Seventh-day Adventists to hold our ground of "sola scriptura"—the Bible and the Bible only—to preserve the unity of our Church. Does biblical evidence exist for the ordination of women? In this straightforward and well-documented writing, the Wahlens simplify the paradoxical controversy that exists among scholars. This careful study answers important questions of gender-inclusivity and gender-exclusivity through a clear and biblical approach. All can benefit from this in-depth, but lay-oriented, study of Scripture within context and excerpts from the historical writings of the Adventist movement. This must-read book offers fresh insight in a sensible and sensitive manner. The Wahlens have done our Church a great service in writing this.

From: Sikhu Hlatshwayo

Administrator, Center of Adventist Ministry to Public University Students (CAMPUS)

This book is intuitively accessible to any thinking reader. Its value transcends the current debate on the ordination of women to pastoral ministry, to addressing the underlying question of methods of Bible study. In a sense, women's ordination may be viewed as a case study for this book's treatment of how to study the Bible. It argues persuasively that this topic is theological in nature and, as in all matters of faith and practice, that we can find answers in the Bible.

INTRODUCTION: GETTING STARTED

One of the most discussed topics in the Seventh-day Adventist Church today is women's ordination. Studies, lectures, books, articles, and papers by the dozen have been presented on the subject. Scholars, evangelists, administrators, pastors, lay members—all of these have weighed in on the topic. But for all of the time and energy devoted, there still seems to be no clear answer to the question as to whether or not women should be ordained to the gospel ministry. Why is that?

How can it be that Seventh-day Adventist theologians today cannot agree on this question? Some scholars say it's a theological/biblical question, while others suggest it's not a theological question at all but is instead a purely ecclesiological matter (that is, dealing with how the church operates).

But shouldn't everything we do as a church (ecclesiology) be based on the Bible (theology)? As Seventh-day Adventists, we are a Bible-based movement; therefore, our church practices flow out of our theology and cannot really be separated from it. If we should try to pull apart these two inseparable things, would we not risk damaging both?

Throughout the history of the Seventh-day Adventist Church, whenever a perplexing problem has arisen, the answer has been found through prayer and study of God's Word—the Bible. Why should the question of women's ordination be any different?

"All Scripture is given by inspiration of God, and is profitable for doctrine, for reproof, for correction, for instruction in righteousness, that the man of God may be complete, thoroughly equipped for every good work" (2 Tim. 3:16).

If this is important for us as individuals, how much more important it is for us as a church! God promises to guide us, so we can be confident of discovering His wisdom on this topic, too:

"I will instruct you and teach you in the way you should go; I will guide you with My eye" (Ps. 32:8).

"If any of you lacks wisdom, let him ask of God, who gives to all liberally and without reproach, and it will be given to him. But let him ask in faith, with no doubting, for he who doubts is like a wave of the sea driven and tossed by the wind" (James 1:5, 6).

"All the words of my mouth are with righteousness; nothing crooked or perverse is in them. They are all plain to him who understands, and right to those who find knowledge" (Prov. 8:8, 9).

God has not left us as orphans (John 14:18, Matt. 7:7), without direction. For every question, God has an answer. In Psalm 119:105 we read, "Your word is a lamp to my feet and a light to my path."

We invite you to prayerfully join us as we search God's Word for His answers.

—Clinton and Gina Wahlen, April 2015

ONE

SAME BIBLE, DIFFERENT ANSWERS

S he and I sat across the table from each other, making chit-chat until our lunch was served. Finally, she blurted out her question: "Why do Adventists go to church on Saturday, when Jesus' disciples and all New Testament Christians worship on Sunday?"

It was an honest question. My friend was a Bible-believing Christian who loved Jesus, believed in the power of prayer, and ministered together with her pastor-husband at a small interdenominational church. We had a lot in common.

As I attempted to share biblical reasons for keeping the Sabbath, she brought up New Testament passages such as Matthew 28:1, Acts 20:7, 1 Corinthians 16:1, 2, and Revelation 1:10, which to her showed that Sunday is "the Lord's Day" and was indeed the new day of worship. Inevitably, we could not come to an agreement.

How could two young women who both loved Jesus with all of their hearts, believed the Bible was God's Word, and were dedicated to sharing the good news of the gospel with the world, come to such different conclusions regarding this seemingly simple question?

Did the fact that we came up with different answers to the question, in spite of both of us using the Bible for our answers, mean that the Bible didn't actually provide a definitive, culturally applicable, relevant answer to our question?

Indeed, biblical scholars and theologians have thoroughly studied this question and haven't come to an agreement. Although the overwhelming majority admit that the Bible doesn't have a lot to say about Sunday, some texts appear to indicate that Sunday is the day on which Christians should go to church.

One Bible—Different Answers

So, one Bible, different answers. What does it mean?

▶ That the Bible doesn't have a clear answer when scholars don't agree?

▶ That the subject must not be very important?

▶ That we should determine the answer from something else, such as culture?

These same arguments have been applied to the question of women's ordination. Because Bible scholars and theologians have not come to an agreement, some claim this shows that the Bible doesn't give a clear answer to this question. Others say that the Bible is actually very clear when everything bearing on the topic is considered together.

Nothing is new here about these questions. Back in 1990, Dr. Gerhard F. Hasel, long-time dean of the Seventh-day Adventist Theological Seminary at Andrews University, wrote:

> Should the Bible give direction to all teachings, the full belief system, the entire lifestyle and policies that Adventists stand for, or should the Bible be used only to some degree, or not be used at all when interpretations differ?[1]

Then, referring to a study on women's ordination that had recently been completed (1989), Dr. Hasel continued:

> It is both amazing and disturbing that the chairperson of a major commission studying a divisive issue in the Adventist church recently concluded that, inasmuch as some of the

papers of experts studying biblical aspects of the topic diverged in their conclusions, these papers canceled one another out and the Bible offers no 'thus saith the Lord' on the matter as a basis for a denominational decision.[2]

Dr. Hasel then poses an important question:

But does it really follow when experts disagree on their interpretations of biblical evidence that the Bible cannot be used to decide a question? Is it not rather mandatory, when divergence of interpretations exists, that we inquire as to the hermeneutical methods that the experts are using and what presuppositions are at work?[3]

Approaches Determine Answers

Let's return to the situation my Sunday-keeping friend and I faced when we reached different conclusions about Sabbath and Sunday. Could it be that the reason we didn't agree was that our "hermeneutical methods and presuppositions"—that is, the way we approached the reading and understanding of the Bible—were different, and our methods determined the outcome?

For example, most Sunday-keeping Christians will:

▸ focus on a few selected passages from the New Testament (as my friend did), and ignore other texts that don't agree with their presuppositions.

▸ read the above passages as if they are supporting Sunday-keeping, when in reality they have nothing to do with keeping a day of worship.

▸ ignore clear passages of Scripture that support the seventh-day Sabbath.

▸ claim that because there isn't a prescription in the New Testament to keep the Sabbath holy and there appears to be a command not to judge those who don't (Col. 2:16), it must be a cultural and ceremonial relic of the Old Testament that was done away with at the Cross.

In short, we can see that one hermeneutical method used to support Sunday-keeping is to: (a) limit the texts to a few, unclear passages; (b) ignore clear passages not in support of their presupposition; (c) claim that lack of clear evidence in the New Testament to keep the Sabbath holy means God must not require it.

Seventh-day Adventist Approach to Scripture

On the other hand, as Seventh-day Adventists, our approach to biblical interpretation has always been to:

▶ "Seek to grasp the simple, most obvious meaning of the biblical passage being studied."

▶ "Recognize that the Bible is its own best interpreter and that the meaning of words, expressions, and whole passages is best determined by diligently comparing scripture with scripture."

▶ "Study the context of the passage under consideration by relating it to the sentences and paragraphs immediately preceding and following it."

▶ Understand as far as possible "the historical circumstances in which the passage was written."

▶ Notice "the grammar and sentence construction in order to discover the author's meaning."

▶ "Explore the historical and cultural factors" in connection with the biblical text.

▶ Recognize that Ellen G. White's "expositions on any given Bible passage offer an inspired guide to the meaning of texts without exhausting their meaning or preempting the task of exegesis" (that is, careful study of the passage).[4]

In addition, as Seventh-day Adventists, we see the Scriptures as having both a human and a divine element—meaning that God didn't dictate the Bible word for word; instead, "holy men of God spoke as they were moved by the Holy Spirit" (1 Pet. 1:21).

We also believe that "the Bible is its own best interpreter and when studied as a whole it depicts a consistent, harmonious truth," and that while it was originally given to those who lived in the ancient world, "the Bible transcends its cultural backgrounds to serve as God's Word for all cultural, racial, and situational contexts in all ages."[5]

Methods and the Debate

So what does this have to do with the current debate over women's ordination? A lot, as we will soon see.

Why is it that even though, since the 1970s, numerous study commissions and other groups—most recently the Theology of Ordination Study Committee—have grappled with this issue, there still has been no resolution to this question? Is it simply because scholars cannot agree on the issue? Is it because the Bible has no clear answer? Or could it be, as Dr. Gerhard Hasel suggested, that the answer to resolving this stalemate might be in the way we approach the Bible itself and how we understand its meaning?

Endnotes:

1. Gerhard F. Hasel, "The Crisis of the Authority of the Bible As the Word of God," *Journal of the Adventist Theological Society*, vol. 1, no. 1 (1990), 16.

2. Ibid.

3. Ibid., 16, 17.

4. "Methods of Bible Study," approved by the Executive Committee of the General Conference of Seventh-day Adventists at the Annual Council, Rio de Janeiro, Brazil, October 12, 1986, http://www.adventist.org/en/information/official-statements/documents/article/go/0/methods-of-bible-study/ (accessed March 19, 2015).

5. Ibid.

TWO

IS ORDINATION BIBLICAL?

M any people have wondered why the topic of ordination has become such a big deal. Some have asserted that ordination is not a biblical concept but is simply a church practice. Since it is a church practice, they argue, questions related to it can be decided on a policy level, like other practical matters. Others claim that ordination is biblical and that the Bible provides both theological and practical answers regarding its origins, qualifications for ordained offices, and even how an ordination ceremony is to proceed.

To be sure, you won't find a "Thou shalt ordain," or "Thou shalt not ordain" listed among the Ten Commandments. But then, many biblical commands aren't found in the Ten Commandments. For example, what about Jesus' command to follow His example in washing each other's feet, and His command in connection with the Lord's Supper, "Do this in remembrance of Me" (1 Cor. 11:24)? Or the Great Commission to "Go, and make disciples . . ." (Matt. 28:19)? These aren't part of the Ten Commandments, but they're still commands. They are not optional.

But is ordination biblical? Can we find this practice within the pages of Scripture?

It is interesting to note that, while the Theology of Ordination Study Committee members weren't able to agree on whether or not women should be ordained to the gospel ministry, they overwhelmingly agreed on ordination itself being a biblical practice. By a vote of 86 to 8, they approved a Consensus Statement on the "Theology of Ordination."[1] To summarize a few points of the statement:

Ordination is a biblical practice, setting apart ministers who oversee the Church when they meet the scriptural qualifications.

The New Testament identifies two categories of ordained leaders: 1) elders, including "supervising" elders who oversee multiple congregations, and 2) deacons.

Some individuals are to be ordained for "global church ministry."[2]

But let's not just take their word for it. Let's consider the biblical evidence by following the historical timeline of when these offices first appear in the New Testament.

I. Jesus Establishes His Church

While still on earth, Jesus created a new structure for His Church that centered on the active involvement of every member and a system of servant leadership based on the processes of calling, gifting, and ordaining.

Jesus formally established the structure for His Church by ordaining twelve of His disciples as apostles. These twelve men were set apart from a much larger group of His disciples to form a new beginning for God's people. Mark tells us that Jesus "went up on the mountain and called to Him those whom He desired, and they came to him. And he appointed twelve (whom he also named apostles) so that they might be with Him and He might send them out to preach" (Mark 3:13, 14).

God's calling comes first. Later, after accepting the call to be followers of Jesus and being baptized (see John 4:1, 2), some people are "appointed" or "ordained" for more specific tasks.[3]

After praying all night and considering whom He should choose, Jesus ordained twelve (Luke 6:2-16). He set them apart for the work to which He had called them.

In a chapter of *The Desire of Ages* titled, "He Ordained Twelve," Ellen White gives us a wonderful view of this very special ordination service:

> The first step was now to be taken in the organization of the church that after Christ's departure was to be His representative on earth. No costly sanctuary was at their command, but the Saviour led His disciples to the retreat He loved, and in their minds the sacred experiences of that day were forever linked with the beauty of mountain and vale and sea. . . .

> Their office was the most important to which human beings had ever been called, and was second only to that of Christ Himself. They were to be workers together with God for the saving of the world. As in the Old Testament the twelve patriarchs stand as representatives of Israel, so the twelve apostles were to stand as representatives of the gospel church. . . .

> When Jesus had ended His instruction to the disciples, He gathered the little band close about Him, and kneeling in the midst of them, and laying His hands upon their heads, He offered a prayer dedicating them to His sacred work. Thus the Lord's disciples were ordained to the gospel ministry.[4]

It's interesting that these twelve disciples were ordained more than a year after Jesus first called them to "follow Me" (see Mark 1:16-20; John 1:35-51).[5] Their ordination represents a further stage in their experience as disciples and in the development of the Church. These two levels of discipleship (calling and ordination) are described in John 15:16, where Jesus explains to His disciples: "You did not choose me, but I chose you and appointed you that you should go and bear fruit." In Mark 3:13, 14, this process is described in an abbreviated way. Jesus calls and then ordains His disciples so that He can send them out on His mission.

While the New Testament mentions other groups of disciples, such as "the seventy," Jesus selected and ordained the twelve apostles to leadership in the Church and entrusted them with responsibilities not given to others who followed Him.

A comparison of the several lists we find in Scripture of the twelve apostles (Matt. 10:2-4; Mark 3:16-19; Luke 6:14-16; Acts 1:13) reveals an even more detailed Church organization designed by Jesus.

12 Apostles			
Matt. 10:2-4	Mark 3:16-19	Luke 6:13-16	Acts 1:13
Simon	**Simon**	**Simon**	**Simon**
Andrew	James	Andrew	John
James	John	James	James
John	Andrew	John	Andrew
Philip	**Philip**	**Philip**	**Philip**
Bartholomew	Bartholomew	Bartholomew	Thomas
Thomas	Matthew	Matthew	Bartholomew
Matthew	Thomas	Thomas	Matthew
James, Son of Alphaeus	**James, Son of Alphaeus**	**James, Son of Alphaeus**	**James, Son of Alphaeus**
Thaddaeus	Thaddaeus	Simon the Zealot	Simon the Zealot
Simon the Zealot	Simon the Zealot	Judas Son of James	Judas Son of James
Judas Iscariot	Judas Iscariot	Judas Iscariot	

Notice that the only names occupying the same position in all four lists are Peter, Philip, and James (the son of Alphaeus) and that these three names neatly fall into three subgroups, each consisting of two pairs of disciples. This organized grouping makes it easy to see the way in which Jesus sent the disciples out two by two. Each "two-two" group (which is literally how Mark 6:7 describes it) is headed by one of these three disciples. Interestingly, Ellen White seems to have been aware of this subgrouping: "At the head of one of the groups into which the apostles are divided stands the name of Philip. He was the first disciple to whom Jesus addressed the distinct command, 'Follow Me.'"[6]

After His death and resurrection, Jesus gave the Holy Spirit to the twelve apostles, making them His undershepherds, providing further guidance for them, and authorizing them to act on His behalf (John 20:21-23). He also promised an even greater outpouring of the Spirit to all His disciples—women and men—so that, through the Holy Spirit, Jesus' presence with His church would continue and deepen.

2. Ordination of Deacons

The second example of ordination in the New Testament is recorded in Acts 6. The Christian Church was growing rapidly, and in Jerusalem some complaints arose regarding unfairness in distributing aid to widows in the church.

The twelve apostles called the first church business meeting (see Acts 6:2), and presented the situation to the "multitude of disciples," encouraging them to "seek out from among you seven men of good reputation, full of the Holy Spirit and wisdom, whom we may appoint over this business" (vs. 3).

The plan pleased everyone, and soon seven men were chosen, "whom they set before the apostles: and when they had prayed, they laid hands on them" (vs. 7). This act of ordination represented the setting apart of these men by the apostles to the special role that they had been called to fill, based on the criteria specified by them in verse 3. The required qualifications for deacons are given in more detail by Paul (see 1 Tim. 3:8-10, 12). The apostles, on the other hand, continued to devote themselves "continually to prayer and to the ministry of the word" (Acts 6:4).

Ellen White comments regarding the appointing of deacons in the early church:

> That this step was in the order of God, is revealed in the immediate results for good that were seen. "The word of God increased; and the number of the disciples multiplied in Jerusalem greatly; and a great company of the priests were obedient to the faith." This ingathering of souls was due both to the greater freedom secured by the apostles and to the zeal and power shown by the seven deacons. The fact that these brethren had been ordained for the special work of looking after the needs of the poor, did not exclude them from teaching

the faith. On the contrary, they were fully qualified to instruct others in the truth, and they engaged in the work with great earnestness and success.[7]

3. Ordination of Elders

The third ordained office—that of local church elder—first appears in Acts 11:30. Before this, as we saw in Acts 6, the apostles were the spiritual leaders in the Church. But as a result of persecution, many of the original members of the Jerusalem church were forced to flee (Acts 8:1). Although the apostles remained as long as possible, the persecution intensified to the point that they too had to leave, so they ordained elders to spiritual leadership in Jerusalem. As Luke notes, it was about this time that James the son of Zebedee was martyred and Peter was put in prison (Acts 12:1-4). Peter would have met the same fate if he had not been miraculously delivered by an angel (vss. 5-11).

This practice of ordaining elders as spiritual leaders was also followed by Paul and Barnabas in the churches they established (Acts 14:23). By the time the Jerusalem Council met to discuss whether Gentile believers had to be circumcised in order to be saved and fully accepted into Church fellowship, we see the apostles and elders from Jerusalem and Antioch (and no doubt other places also) meeting together to decide the issue (Acts 15:1-6). Once the decision had been made, it was communicated by means of a letter from the apostles and elders to the churches (vs. 23).

Later, we see Paul giving detailed instructions regarding the qualifications for the office of local elder (or "overseer") to Timothy and also to Titus (1 Tim. 3:2-7; Titus 1:6-10). These men worked with Paul as co-workers in ministry, preaching the gospel in new areas and raising up churches (Acts 16:1-3; 1 Cor. 16:10; 2 Cor. 8:23), and ordaining local elders to oversee them (1 Tim. 5:17; Titus 1:4, 5; James 5:14).

Both Timothy and Titus, because they worked so closely with Paul, traveled widely and were ordained to a wider sphere of ministry. We know that Timothy was ordained by Paul himself, who mentions that he was assisted in the ordination ceremony by a group of elders (1 Tim. 4:14; 2 Tim. 1:6).

Timothy stayed in Ephesus to follow up Paul's work there, while Titus did the same on the island of Crete. By the time Paul wrote his second letter to Timothy, Titus had already moved on to Dalmatia on the eastern shore of the Adriatic Sea (2 Tim. 4:10). Since these men were given supervision over several churches, they can be referred to as "supervising elders" to distinguish them from local church elders.

Ordination is Biblically Based

As we have traced through the history of the early Christian Church, we can see that ordination to ministry began with Jesus Himself ordaining the twelve apostles as the leaders of His Church. We have seen that, as the Church grew, a variety of other leaders were needed for the Church, including deacons, and local church elders, along with "supervising" elders, whom we refer to today as ministers or pastors. Men appointed to each of these offices were ordained—set apart to serve—by the laying on of hands.

What About Deaconesses?

Although women most certainly played an important role in the early Church, the term *deaconess* is not used to describe these women; in fact, the term is not found anywhere in Scripture. In the New Testament, only offices requiring ordination—apostle, deacon, and elder—are mentioned. Deaconesses are discussed further in Chapter 11, "More Questions and Answers."

Endnotes:

1. See "Study Committee Votes Consensus Statement on 'Theology of Ordination,'" *Adventist Review* [Aug. 15, 2013], page 8), http://news.adventist.org/all-news/news/go/2013-07-23/study-committee-votes-consensus-statement-on-theology-of-ordination/

(accessed March 19, 2015).

2. For the full statement, see Appendix 1, "Consensus Statement on a Seventh-day Adventist Theology of Ordination."

3. See Mark 3:14; Acts 1:22; 14:23; 1 Tim. 2:7; and Titus 1:5 in the King James Version. Different Greek words are used with the different aspects of ordination being highlighted: (1) Mark's description that Jesus "made" (*poieō*) the twelve disciples apostles (Mark 3:14) focuses on the creation of this new office. The same word is used in Heb. 3:2 of Jesus having been "made" or "appointed" by God as Apostle and High Priest (which was new in the sense that it was according to the order of Melchizedek rather than Aaron, as Heb. 7:11 explains). Interestingly, the Septuagint of 1 Kings 12:31 and 13:33 use the same verb for the false priests created by Jereboam; (2) This word is not used in Acts 1:22, because the office had already been created by Jesus. Matthias simply "became" (*ginomai*) the twelfth apostle to replace Judas Iscariot. (3) The word in Acts 14:23 focuses on the act of setting elders apart through the "laying on of hands" (*cheirotoneō*). (4) In 1 Tim. 2:7, Paul describes his actual appointment or ordination with the same root word (*tithēmi*) as the terms used elsewhere for the "laying on of hands" (*epitithēmi* in 1 Tim. 5:22 and *epithesis* in 1 Tim. 4:14; 2 Tim. 1:6; Heb. 6:2). (5) The word in Titus 1:5 (as with Heb. 5:1 and 8:3 of the Old Testament priests) means "put in charge" (*kathistēmi*) and focuses on the responsibilities entrusted to ordained elders.

4. Ellen G. White, *The Desire of Ages* (Mountain View, CA: Pacific Press, 1940), 291, 293.

5. The length of time from the disciples' initial call to their being ordained as apostles is clear when comparing the Gospel of John, which records Jesus' ministry in Judea, with the other three Gospels, which focus on the later period in Galilee where Jesus spent most of His time. See *The Seventh-day Adventist Bible Commentary* (ed. Francis D. Nichol; 7 vols.; Washington, D.C.: Review and Herald, 1956), vol. 5, 230-231; cf. 196, 197.

6. White, *The Desire of Ages*, 292.

7. Ellen G. White, *The Acts of the Apostles* (Mountain View, CA: Pacific Press, 1911), 89.

THREE

SOME NOTABLE WOMEN IN THE BIBLE

Throughout the Bible, we meet many notable women, both good and bad. Some were civil leaders, others were prophetesses, many had a very significant influence as mothers.

Influential Women in the Old Testament[1]

The most important mother, of course, is the very first one— Eve, the mother of the human race. Unfortunately, she was also the first sinner and gave the forbidden fruit to Adam, who plunged the world into sin through his transgression (Rom. 5:12; 1 Cor. 15:21, 22). This makes it even more striking that, after God pronounced judgment on sin and affirmed that Adam would suffer death as its inevitable result, Adam describes the woman as the source of all life. In faith, he looks to the future, finds hope in the promise of the woman's seed crushing the serpent's head (Gen. 3:15), and names her "Eve" which means "life" (vs. 20).

Scripture names many other notable mothers. Arguably the most influential mother in Israel was Jochebed. She hid her son Moses in the bulrushes and so successfully educated him during his early years that he "refused to be called the son of Pharoah's daughter, choosing rather to suffer affliction with the people of God" (Heb. 11:24, 25). His older sister Miriam played a key role in facilitating this early childhood education (Exod. 2:7-9). Many years later, she led the women of Israel in a song of victory after crossing the Red Sea. As a prophetess, the words of this song remain on record as witness to God's saving power (15:20, 21). Unfortunately, together with Aaron, she tried to usurp authority that God had given to Moses: "Has the LORD indeed spoken only through Moses? Has he not spoken through us also?" (Num. 12:2). She may have thought that, since she also had the gift of prophecy, she was somehow equal to him in spiritual authority. By afflicting her with leprosy, God indicated that this assumption was not only wrong but sinful. God showed His displeasure toward Aaron by leaving the sanctuary for a time (vss. 9, 10). Interestingly, because of his authority as high priest, Aaron interceded for Miriam along with Moses for her healing (vss. 11-13).

The four daughters of Zelophehad, who were the only children of their father, asked that the land, which would normally be the son's inheritance, be transferred to them. God accepted their petition for fairness: "The daughters of Zelophehad speak what is right; you shall surely give them a possession of inheritance among their father's brothers, and cause the inheritance of their father to pass to them" (Num. 27:7). Furthermore, additional legislation was commanded to clarify the laws of inheritance (vss. 8-11).

A Judge in Israel?

One of the most well-known female leaders of the Old Testament is Deborah. She has been considered not only a prophetess but also a judge. However, the Bible indicates in several important ways that she was not a judge in the same sense as male judges. First, she is never called a "judge," but instead calls herself "a mother in Israel" (Judg. 5:7). She is not raised up by God in the way other judges are (see Judg. 3:9, 15; 6:14; 11:29; 13:24, 25). Nor is the usual way of identifying how long a judge has ruled ("X judged Israel Y years")[2] applied to her.

Instead, the temporary nature of Deborah's judging activity is emphasized in several ways, including use of the phrase *at that time* (4:4) which is not used when referring to judges who are male. This shows that her judging of the people was exceptional and not a regular part of her role as prophetess.

In order to prepare the reader for a woman temporarily acting in this capacity, the way Deborah is introduced deliberately emphasizes in five different ways that she is female—before mentioning her work of judging.[3]

Finally, rather than sitting in the gate as judges and elders did at that time (see Ruth 4:9-11; 1 Sam. 9:18) and as kings did somewhat later (1 Kings 22:10; Jer. 38:7), Deborah is described as sitting under a palm tree between Ramah and Bethel (Judg. 4:5), a place more in line with her role as a prophetic messenger. Ellen White also comments on Deborah's role: "In the absence of the usual magistrates, the people had sought to her for counsel and justice."[4]

Extension of Prophetic Role

Throughout the story of Deborah we find confirmation that her activity was more an extension of her role as a prophet because Barak, the divinely intended judge, was unwilling to lead. Through Deborah's prophetic message (Judg. 4:6), God calls Barak to act as Israel's deliverer. Barak, however, refuses to lead Israel into battle unless Deborah goes with him to "support his efforts by her influence and counsel."[5] Deborah prophesies that she will go and the victory will be gained, but that it "will not lead to your glory, for the Lord will sell Sisera into the hand of a woman" (Jael, not Deborah, vss. 8, 9). The "Song of Deborah," sung by Deborah and Barak, alludes to both of them as "leaders" who took the "lead in Israel" (5:1, 2).

In short, Deborah was obedient to the prophetic role that God had appointed her to do in an exceptional situation. Her work was temporarily expanded to include some of the functions of a judge, but, as Ellen G. White indicates, it was Barak who "had been *designated by the Lord himself* as the one chosen to deliver Israel."[6] This understanding regarding the role of Deborah is confirmed by the New Testament, which mentions Barak, not Deborah, in recalling Israel's deliverance at that time (Heb. 11:32).

Women and Jesus' Ministry

Jesus came to save, to restore in people the image of God. We know from the Gospels (see Matt. 8:5-13; 19:13-26) that a very important part of Jesus' work was breaking down barriers between people. He wanted to break down these barriers so that everyone might join together as one unified Church. As Paul describes it: "For as many of you as were baptized into Christ have put on Christ. There is neither Jew nor Greek, there is neither slave nor free, there is neither male nor female; for you are all one in Christ Jesus" (Gal. 3:27, 28).

It's important to remember that even though it went against the culture of the time, Jesus called women, as well as men, to play important roles within His church. While it is true that Jesus called twelve men to be His apostles, He had many other disciples, including a number of prominent women. These women played very important supportive roles in the ministry of Jesus, including giving financial support, encouragement, and being His witnesses.

Women As Disciples

For example, Luke mentions Mary, the sister of Martha, as sitting at Jesus' feet as a disciple (Luke 10:38, 39), as well as several women who traveled with Jesus in Galilee and supported Him financially: "Now it came to pass, afterward, that He went through every city and village, preaching and bringing the glad tidings of the kingdom of God. And the twelve were with Him, and certain women who had been healed of evil spirits and infirmities—Mary called Magdalene out of whom had come seven demons, and Joanna, who with her husband belonged to the elite few at the very top of the social ladder. In addition to these women that we don't hear much about, but who were vital for enabling Jesus and the apostles to carry on full-time ministry, the previous verse (Luke 8:2) singles out Mary Magdalene for special mention as having been freed from the seven demons who had controlled her. The other women too, it says, were either delivered from demon possession as was Mary, or healed of disease and, apparently in gratitude, gave generous financial support and encouragement to Jesus' ministry.

Mary Magdalene is mentioned again as being present at the crucifixion, together with other women, including another Mary and

Salome, who followed Jesus and ministered to Him when He was in Galilee (Mark 15:40, 41). These women, after the Sabbath had ended, bought spices and early on Sunday morning went to the tomb to anoint Jesus' body but found the tomb empty. An angel commanded them to tell the disciples that Jesus had risen from the dead and would meet them in Galilee. According to Matthew, the women saw Jesus, who commanded them to tell the disciples that He was alive. It is significant that Jesus appeared to them, even before the apostles, making these believing women the first witnesses of His resurrection (Matt. 28:9, 10).

The fact that the resurrected Jesus appeared first to women followers was amazing—it went against the entire Jewish social, cultural, and educational structures. It didn't make any sense to the apostles, and when the women brought the news that Jesus had risen, they weren't able to bring themselves to believe their witness (see Luke 24:9-11). They needed the gift of the Holy Spirit and to be witnesses themselves so that they, along with the women disciples, might *as a whole Church* be the complete witness the world needs.

The Day of Pentecost

After Jesus' ascension, Acts 2 records that all of the believers were together praying on the day of Pentecost, waiting for the promised baptism of the Holy Spirit in obedience to the Lord's command (Luke 24:49; Acts 1:5, 8). They were "all with one accord in one place" (Acts 2:1) when the Holy Spirit was poured out. Women as well as men began speaking with power and conviction.

Peter, again speaking for the group, identified this outpouring as a fulfillment of prophecy: "And it shall come to pass in the last days, says God, that I will pour out my Spirit on all flesh; your sons and your daughters shall *prophesy*, your young men shall see visions, your old men shall dream dreams; and on My menservants and maidservants I will pour out my Spirit in those days, and they shall *prophesy* (Acts 2:17, 18, quoting Joel 2:28, 29).

Notice how the text quoted from Joel talks about men and women receiving visions and dreams and *prophesying*. Jesus also spoke of sending prophets to bear witness about Him (Matt. 23:34; Luke

11:49). The New Testament confirms that the prophetic gift came upon both men and women and was active throughout the time of the apostles. In the book of Acts, several of these prophets are mentioned: Agabus (11:27, 28; 21:10), Barnabas and others (13:1), Judas and Silas (15:32) and the four daughters of Philip (21:9), besides those in Ephesus upon whom the gift of tongues came (19:6). In fact, throughout Scripture the gift of prophecy comes upon both women and men. Those mentioned in the Old Testament as having this gift include such women as Miriam (Exod. 15:20), Deborah (Judg. 4:4), Huldah (2 Kings 22:14; 2 Chr. 34:22), Noadiah (Neh. 6:14), and the wife of Isaiah (Isa. 9:3).

More Women in the New Testament

We also have ample evidence that in the New Testament Church women worked in various capacities within local congregations. For example, Priscilla and her husband Aquila, who in their spare time worked with Paul in Corinth, Ephesus, and Rome, taught accurately "the way of God." In addition, Aquila and Priscilla opened their home for church gatherings (Acts 18:1, 18, 26; 1 Cor. 16:9; Rom. 16:3).

In the New Testament, other prominent women, such as Mary of Jerusalem (mother of John Mark) and Lydia of Philippi (see Acts 12:12; 16:15), are also mentioned as hosting Christian gatherings.

In Romans 16, Paul gives greetings to a long list of believers, including many women. Phoebe, a "servant" (*diakonos* in Greek) or helper[7] of the church at Cenchrea near Corinth and possible patron of Paul and others, delivered Paul's epistle to Rome and may have encouraged generous support of his mission to Spain (Rom. 16:1; 15:28).[8] Other women mentioned here by Paul include Mary, who was well-known for her hard work in the church in Rome (vs. 6); Tryphaena, Tryphosa, and the "beloved" Persis, who "worked hard in the Lord" (vs. 12); and many others.

Paul's mention of "Junia" (as the name is rendered in some recent translations)[9] has occasioned quite a bit of discussion. Assuming Paul refers to a woman, Andronicus and Junia would then most likely be a husband and wife team like Aquila and Priscilla. Even if this is correct, which is not completely clear,[10] the most that we can say about this pair is that they were "well-known to the apostles" (vs. 7, ESV),[11] not that they were apostles.[12] While there were many followers of Jesus, it was the Twelve (including Matthias, Acts 1:26) who were known as "*the* apostles" in the early period to which Paul here refers ("they were in Christ before I was," i.e., before A.D. 34).

Active Supporters

Throughout the Bible, women fill important roles.[13] In both the Old and New Testaments, they are called directly by God to deliver His message as prophetesses. Notable among these is Deborah, who in extraordinary circumstances at the time of the Judges, was sought by people to decide their cases and played a key supportive role when Barak led Israel into battle. In the New Testament, we see them actively supporting the work of Jesus by following Him, giving of their means, and lending their influence. Women were also involved in the work of the early Church. Paul mentions several women who assisted him. Some, like Priscilla, with her husband Aquila, opened their homes for church meetings.

However, nowhere in the Bible do we see women filling any ordained leadership roles. No woman is ever mentioned serving as a priest, apostle, elder, or deacon.[14] Is this a result of cultural prejudice? Might God have wanted women to serve in these spiritual leadership roles from the beginning? What does the Bible say about God's will regarding Church leadership today?

Endnotes:

1. See also the excellent overview by Laurel Damsteegt, "Women of the Old Testament: Women of Influence" (paper presented at the Theology of Ordination Study Committee, Linthicum Heights, Md., July 2013), https://www.adventistarchives.org/women-of-the-old-testament.pdf (accessed March 30, 2015).

2. For examples of this formula, see Judges 10:2, 3; 12:7, 9, etc.

3. For a more detailed discussion, see Edwin Reynolds and Clinton Wahlen, "Minority Report," in *North American Division Theology of Ordination Study Committee Report* (November 2013), p. 201, http://static.squarespace.com/static/50d0ebebe4b0ceb6af5fd-d33/t/527970c2e4b039a2e8329354/1383690434980/nad-ordina-tion-14-minority.pdf (March 19, 2015).

4. Ibid.

5. Ibid., par. 6.

6. Ibid. (emphasis supplied).

7. Throughout the New Testament, *diakonos* (translated "servant"), is the preferred designation for all church workers regardless of who they were, because all are serving Christ, who made Himself a Servant. For more examples of this use, see Mark 10:45; John 12:26; 2 Tim. 1:18; Heb. 6:10. In other places, *diakonos* is used in the technical sense of "deacon"—a church officer who works under the authority of an elder/overseer (Phil. 1:1; 1 Tim. 3:8, 12). The deacons in 1 Timothy 3 are in apparent contrast to the "women" who seem to have fulfilled some official church duties without an official title (vs. 11). These two basic offices appear to be referred to also in 1 Peter 4:10, 11: some should speak "as the oracles of God" (elders), while others should "minister" or "serve" (using the verb *diakoneō*) "with the ability which God supplies."

8. In the last part of Romans 16:1, Paul adds that Phoebe "has been a helper of many and of myself also." The Greek word here translated "helper" (*prostatis*) is widely understood as referring to her as a financial supporter of Paul and others. The suggestion that here it means "leader" is based on a usage of the word several centuries earlier and does not fit the context of this verse, as it is difficult to imagine Paul considering Phoebe as his "leader," something he refused to concede even to other apostles (2 Cor. 11:5; 12:11), including James, Peter, and John (Gal. 2:6-10).

9. E.g., NRSV, ESV, and NKJV. The 2011 edition of the NIV renders the name Junia, while the 1984 NIV rendered it with the masculine name Junias (which is how the RSV, NASB [1977, 1995], and WEB render it). The possibility of this person being a man is also acknowledged by other versions in the marginal notes (e.g., ESV, NET).

10. Appealing to instances of the *Latin* name "Junia" hardly proves that the Greek form of the name mentioned here in Paul's epistle is the same name because the ending could be either masculine or feminine and, in fact, the same ending (-*as*) occurs in other clearly masculine names in Romans 16.

11. Some translations render this phrase well-known to or outstanding "*among* the apostles," although the NIV11 marginal note admits it may also be translated "are esteemed by [the apostles]."

12. See Richard Sabuin, "Were Andronicus and Iounian apostles?" *Ministry*, vol. 86, no. 5 (May 2014), 10-13.

13. See the chapters, "Women of Note in the Old Testament" and "Women of Note in the New Testament," in Ellen G. White, *Daughters of God* (Hagerstown, MD: Review and Herald, 2005), 21-76.

14. Further on the reasons for Phoebe not being considered either a "deacon(ess)" or a church leader, see Chapter 11, "More Questions and Answers," under "Questions About Specific Bible Passages," Question 7 on Romans 16:1, 2.

FOUR

THE HUSBAND OF ONE WIFE...REALLY?

A n important question to consider at this point is this: Does the Bible give a clear answer as to who may be ordained to serve in Church leadership roles? In other words, are there clear biblical qualifications for these spiritual leadership positions, and do those qualifications still apply worldwide in the Church today? These questions are at the heart of the debate over women's ordination.

As we saw in Chapter 1, hermeneutical approaches (the ways we read the Bible) make a big difference in the answers that we find within Scripture. In Chapter 2 it became clear that ordination is a biblical practice and that the New Testament identifies two categories of ordained church leaders: (1) elder and (2) deacon. The New Testament category of "elder" is broader than what we sometimes think of today. It includes ministers, like Timothy and Titus who traveled widely and supervised churches over a large area (1 Tim. 4:14; Titus 1:5), and even apostles, who refer to themselves with this title (1 Pet. 5:1; 2 John 1; 3 John 1).

Biblical Authority

As we seek Bible answers regarding who may be ordained to leadership in the Church, it's important to determine who, or what, we consider to be a reliable and authoritative source. Our view of the Bible's authority is crucial because that will ultimately determine what we accept (or reject).

In a paper titled, "Biblical Authority, Hermeneutics, and the Role of Women," Dr. Gerhard Hasel explains, "Basically there are but two positions on the authority of the Bible. One position maintains the full and unlimited authority of the Bible without qualification and the other holds to some kind of limited authority of the Bible."[1]

When we read the Bible, and especially when approaching seemingly controversial passages, the way we understand Scripture and its authority will greatly impact our conclusions.

Understanding Scripture

In this book, we take the official Church position that "the Bible is its own best interpreter and when studied as a whole it depicts a consistent, harmonious truth." Although originally written to people in the ancient world, it "transcends its cultural backgrounds to serve as God's Word for all cultural, racial, and situational contexts in all ages."[2]

This doesn't mean that we can't gain useful information from outside the Bible. "Archaeology, anthropology, and history may contribute to understanding the meaning of the text,"[3] but it will supplement and enlarge upon the historical and cultural information that can be gleaned from the Bible itself, rather than challenge or overthrow it.[4]

It is an interesting fact that the New Testament lists qualifications for all ordained offices: apostle (Acts 1:21, 22), deacon (Acts 6:3; 1 Tim. 3:8-10, 12), and the elder/minister who oversees the church (1 Tim. 3:2-7; Titus 1:5-9). Let's look at the biblical qualifications for the elder/minister in more detail.

Paul's Epistles to Ministers

The books of 1 and 2 Timothy are letters written by an aging Paul to a young minister, whom Paul was preparing as a leader of the Church after he was gone. Paul's letters to Timothy are given as instructions for an effective ministry—in Ephesus where Timothy happened to be located at the time, but also more broadly as guidance for him wherever he might labor, as well as for the church in general.

The same is true of the letter to Titus. He, like Timothy, was a co-worker of Paul. At the time Paul wrote to him, he was working on the island of Crete, but by the time Paul wrote his second letter to Timothy, Titus had already left the churches on Crete in the hands of the elders he had ordained (as Paul instructed him to do in Titus 1:5) and had moved on to Dalmatia.

As is typical for letters written by Paul, the subject of 1 Timothy is made clear from the beginning—to strengthen the Church. It's interesting that in this connection, Paul refers to God's management plan for the Church—known as *oikonomia* in Greek. "*Oikonomia* refers to the organization and ordering of a household or the responsibility of management that maintains order" (as used in 1 Cor. 9:17; Col. 1:25).[5] This fits well with the description of the Church being the "household of God" (1 Tim. 3:15). Other translations for *oikonomia* include, "God's way of ordering things"[6] and "the good order from God" (1 Tim. 1:4, ESV, margin).

Significantly, Paul describes the overseer (or elder) as the one who "manages God's household" (Titus 1:7, NIV11; *oikonomos theou* in Greek). We also see this managerial description of an elder in 1 Corinthians 4:1, 2.

Biblical Qualifications for Overseers

So what are the qualifications given for the elder/gospel minister who oversees or manages God's household, the church? We find the answer in two Bible passages.

1 Timothy 3:2-7, NAS95. An overseer, then, must be above reproach, the husband of one wife, temperate, prudent, respectable, hospitable, able to teach, not addicted to wine or pugnacious, but gentle, peaceable, free from the love of money. He must be one who manages his own household well, keeping his children under control with all dignity (but if a man does not know how to manage his own household, how will he take care of the church of God?), and not a new convert, so that he will not become conceited and fall into the condemnation incurred by the devil. And he must have a good reputation with those outside the church, so that he will not fall into reproach and the snare of the devil.

Titus 1:5-9, NAS95. For this reason I left you in Crete, that you would set in order what remains and appoint elders in every city as I directed you, namely, if any man is above reproach, the husband of one wife, having children who believe, not accused of dissipation or rebellion. For the overseer must be above reproach as God's steward, not self-willed, not quick-tempered, not addicted to wine, not pugnacious, not fond of sordid gain, but hospitable, loving what is good, sensible, just, devout, self-controlled, holding fast the faithful word which is in accordance with the teaching, so that he will be able both to exhort in sound doctrine and to refute those who contradict.

Let's consider some important points about these passages:

▸ They were written to two different pastors, rather than to churches (which is why they are referred to as "Pastoral Epistles").

▸ These pastors—Timothy and Titus—were serving in very different areas. Timothy was in Ephesus, one of the largest and most important cities of the Roman world. Titus was on the island of Crete, where there were a number of small towns and villages.

▸ Both Timothy and Titus were traveling ministers/evangelists, having worked in other areas besides those in which they happened to be located at the time 1 Timothy and Titus were written. Later, Titus went to Dalmatia (2 Tim. 4:10). Thus, this counsel would guide them wherever they would be.

▸ In both passages the qualifications for "overseers" are identical.

This chart provides an easy comparison between the two passages:

1 Timothy 3:2-7	Titus 1:5-9
3:2 – An overseer, then, must be ... above reproach, the husband of one wife, temperate, prudent, respectable, hospitable, able to teach,	1:7 – An overseer . . . must be above reproach 1:6 – the husband of one wife 1:8 – self-controlled, . . . disciplined 1:8 – a lover of good 1:8 – upright 1:8 – hospitable 1:7 – He must hold firm to the trustworthy word as taught, so that he may be able to give instruction in sound doctrine and also to rebuke those who contradict it.
3:3 – not addicted to wine [not] pugnacious, gentle, peaceable, free from the love of money.	1:7 – He must not . . . be a drunkard 1:7 – [not] quick-tempered or . . . violent 1:8 – holy 1:7 – [not] greedy for gain,
3:4 – He must be one who manages his own household well, keeping his children under control with all dignity	1:6 – his children are believers and not open to the charge of debauchery or insubordination

A Unique Qualification

Notice that all of the qualifications, except for one, deal with the character of the person that should be an elder. The one qualification that differs from the rest is that the elder/minister "must be the husband of one wife." Might this be significant?

When we consider a person's character, we understand that it is not static—it is (hopefully) dynamic and growing. In other words, there are degrees of character—being temperate, respectable, hospitable, and so on. As a person grows and matures, hopefully these Christian character traits will also become stronger and more evident.[7]

On the other hand, one qualification, "the overseer must be . . . the husband of one wife," is not a matter of degrees—either he is the husband of one wife, or he is not.

The most obvious element of this qualification is that of gender. Unless we would redefine these commonly accepted terms so that a "husband" may be female and a "wife" may be male, most readers of the Bible would naturally understand that the elder/minister overseeing the church must be male.

From Clarity to Uncertainty

Over the past forty years, however, this seemingly obvious conclusion has increasingly been questioned by some biblical scholars. This tendency is evident from the way the Greek phrase of this verse has been translated in some recent versions of the Bible (NAB, NRSV, CEV, and CEB), which replace "husband of one wife" with gender-neutral wording.

How is it that such apparently plain language—which is as clear in Greek as it is in English—can now be read so differently from the way it has been understood across languages and cultures for nearly 2,000 years? Could it be that new methods and new hermeneutical approaches (ways of reading Scripture) have helped make this leap of language possible?

Let's briefly look at some of the common reasons given as to why this text doesn't really mean "the husband of one wife":

1. Lack of Clarity

The suggestion is sometimes made that the text of 1 Timothy 3:2 is not as clear as it sounds. A few argue that the Bible was written from the perspective of a male-dominant society, as evidenced by androcentric language. Speeches in Acts, for example, typically address men, even though women were also present (Acts 1:11, 16; 2:22, etc.). But commands in Greek, the language of the New Testament, are usually gender-neutral, and when it was important to make a distinction in gender, the writers did so (e.g., 1 Cor. 7:16; Eph. 5:22; 1 Pet. 3:1).[8]

Others assert that the text literally says in Greek "one woman man," meaning that the emphasis is on being faithful to one's spouse, rather than being a "husband" or a "man." Actually, the Greek literally says "of one wife husband." The word used for "husband" in Greek is *anēr*. Some suggest that *anēr* can also be used to signify a female, but this is simply not true. Although the word can mean "man" as representative of human beings (only 9 out of 216 uses in the New Testament), Paul never uses it this way. Furthermore, regarding 1 Timothy 3:2, fifty-seven of sixty-one English translations, ranging from the Wycliffe Bible (1382) to the twenty-first century World English Bible, restrict anēr to the male gender; only four give it a gender-neutral sense.[9] See Appendix 2, "English Bible Translations of 1 Timothy 3:2."

So did Paul really mean what he wrote—that the "overseer . . . must be the husband of one wife"? From the wording, which contains both husband and wife in relationship, the immediate literary context of 1 Timothy 3:2 (which moves from gender-inclusive to gender-specific, and finally to gender-exclusive—discussed later in this chapter), as well as from the repetition of qualifications that we find in Titus, it is clear that when using *anēr* here—in agreement with his practice everywhere else—Paul does in fact mean a man, a "husband of one wife."

2. Polygamy/Marital Faithfulness

Another objection is that gender is not the issue here. The text may simply be saying that the overseer (male or female) should not be polygamous; they should have exactly one spouse. Or simpler still, perhaps the text is simply requiring faithfulness to one's spouse. The problem with these suggestions is that polygamy was virtually non-existent in the Roman world of the first century.[10] In fact, there were Roman laws against polygamy, just as there are such laws in many countries today. And if Paul meant only that marital faithfulness should be the qualification, he could have made that clear here in 1 Timothy, just as he does in 1 Corinthians 7:10, 11.

3. Culture, Time, and Place

Another frequent objection is that Paul's instructions have to do only with a specific situation in the church of Ephesus at that time, and that they were never intended for a general application to other churches or for all time. But, as we have seen, the same instructions were given to Titus, who was then working on the island of Crete.[11] Furthermore, unlike Paul's epistles written to *local* churches, the Pastoral Epistles were written to men who worked in *many* churches. It is true that Paul's epistles were written within cultural settings that differ significantly from many cultures today. But that is true of all the books of the Bible. In fact, the Old Testament is even farther removed from our culture and time. But that doesn't mean we can ignore what it says. Many inspired books are mentioned in Scripture that were not included in the Bible (see, for example, 1 Chr. 29:29; 2 Chr. 9:29; Col. 4:16). The likely reason these writings were not included is that they were more limited in their application. If they would have been relevant for our day, certainly God would have insured their preservation within the pages of Scripture. As Paul says, the writings that have been preserved are for us (Rom. 15:4; 1 Cor. 10:11).

"All People"

Of course, when seeking to understand any verse of the Bible, it's helpful to look at the context of the verse. As we consider this passage in 1 Timothy 3, it is helpful to understand the context set forth in the previous chapter. 1 Timothy 2 begins with instructions that prayer should be offered for all people (vs. 1). The phrase *all people* occurs several times in 1 Timothy and seems to be an important emphasis. Prayer is to be offered for all people, because God "desires all people to be saved and to come to the knowledge of the truth" (vs. 4). Christ "gave himself as a ransom for all" (vs. 6). God "is the Savior of all people" (4:10).

These passages in 1 Timothy echo the words found in Galatians 3:28: "There is neither Jew nor Greek, there is neither slave nor free, there is neither male nor female; for you are all one in Christ Jesus." Clearly, Paul is teaching in these passages that salvation is made available to all—on the same basis—without regard to gender. It is with this foundational understanding—that all are equal in Christ through redemption, just as all are equal in the image of God through Creation (Gen. 1:26-28)—that Paul's statements regarding the different contributions of men and women in the Church are to be understood. In addition, it's good to keep in mind that "when the author [Paul] wishes to be gender-specific he uses restrictive terms."[12]

From Gender-Inclusive to Gender-Specific

Paul was very adept at using the Greek language and chose carefully the words he used. Fortunately, we have several examples in 1 Timothy showing Paul using gender-inclusive, gender-specific, and gender-exclusive language.

1. Gender-Inclusive (1 Tim. 2:1-7)

As discussed in the section above regarding Paul's use of "all people," gender-inclusive terms are used repeatedly.

▸ Prayer should be offered for all people (vs. 1).

▸ God desires all people to be saved and come to a knowledge of the truth (vs. 4).

▸ Christ gave Himself as a ransom for all (vs. 6).

2. Gender-Specific (1 Tim. 2:8-15).

Paul turns to gender-specific language in order to explain how men and women should relate to each other in the worship setting.

▸ Men are to take the lead in the church's worship and prayer (vs. 8). Clearly, this does not mean women cannot have important roles in worship, because Paul also refers to women praying and prophesying during the worship service (1 Cor. 11:5).

▸ Women should dress modestly. They shouldn't try to usurp the established teaching authority of the minister who oversees the church (vss. 9-12). We'll discuss this passage further in Chapter 5, "Must Women Keep Silent?"

3. Gender-Exclusive (1 Tim. 3:1-12).

Beginning with the qualifications for church officers in chapter 3, Paul uses even more specific, gender-exclusive language. He doesn't refer to just "anyone," but says, as the more literal NASB translation puts it, "If any man aspires to the office of overseer, it is a fine work he desires to do" (vs. 1).

Next he lists the qualifications for this office: "An overseer, then, must be above reproach, the husband of one wife . . ." (vs. 2).

This is not just gender-specific, it's gender-exclusive, for several reasons:

▸ It is a fixed requirement (meaning it's a yes/no question), that appears three times: here and in Titus 1:6 for overseers/elders, and for deacons in 1 Timothy 3:12.

▸ Women assistants (whom we sometimes call deaconesses) are referred to in vs. 11 as a group separate from both elders and deacons, with a different list of qualifications, so they cannot be included in either of the other categories.

▸ Paul uses the opposite phrase, wife of one husband, in 1 Timothy 5:9, referring to one of the conditions for widows to receive financial help from the congregation (vs. 16). If Paul had intended to be gender-neutral with regard to the qualifications for the elder who oversees the church, he could have combined the two phrases, "the overseer . . . must be the husband of one wife or the wife of one husband." But Paul didn't do this. That means Paul meant what he said.

▸ Paul deals, in order, with smaller and smaller groups: first "all" (gender-inclusive), then "men" and "women" (gender-specific), and finally "husband of one wife" (gender-exclusive).

A Clear Command

"An overseer, then, must be . . . the husband of one wife." Note that Paul says "must" (*dei* in Greek). There are several other ways to express a command in Greek. But this wording, which is the strongest possible command form in Greek, is as clear in that language as it is in English. It is the same "must" used in Mark 13:10—"And the gospel must first be preached to all the nations"; John 3:14—"And as Moses lifted up the serpent in the wilderness, even so must the Son of Man be lifted up"; Acts 23:11, when Jesus told Paul, "you must also bear witness at Rome"; 1 Corinthians 15:53—"For this corruptible must put on incorruption, and this mortal must put on immortality"; 2 Corinthians 5:10—"For we must all appear before the judgment seat of Christ"; Hebrews 11:6—"But without faith it is impossible to please Him, for he who comes to God must believe that He is." These and many other passages show us that this "must" (dei) is not optional. This must is mandatory.

Is the Bible Clear on Who Should Be Ordained?

Let's now return to the questions stated at the beginning of this chapter: Does the Bible give a clear answer as to who may be ordained to serve as overseeing elders of the Church? Are there clear biblical qualifications for these spiritual leadership positions, and do those qualifications still apply to the Church worldwide today? The answer to all of these questions is clearly "Yes." Like the other ordained offices of the New Testament Church, overseeing elders must meet the biblical qualifications specified in Paul's epistles to Timothy and Titus. These standards were upheld by the apostles everywhere elders were ordained (Acts 14:23; Phil. 1:1; Titus 1:5; 1 Pet. 5:1-4).

The stipulation that elders must be the husband of one wife is as clear in Greek as it is in English. If we ever come to the place where we can read this requirement to mean "wife of one husband" or simply "faithful man [or woman]," then we can make any verse of Scripture say whatever we want it to say or whatever the surrounding culture pressures us to make it say. In that case, biblical authority would no longer have the same role in the Church. We are not left to guess what the result would be. We see how it has led only to division and fragmentation within other Christian denominations. As one clergyman in the Anglican Church recently observed, the cause of division is not just the ordination of women or issues of sexuality, but "how attached to the Bible's teachings do we intend to be."[13] As Seventh-day Adventists, our unity has always been a result of our faithfulness to Scripture. And by God's grace that will continue to be our safeguard in the future.

Endnotes:

1. Gerhard F. Hasel, "Biblical Authority, Hermeneutics, and the Role of Women" (paper presented at the Commission on the Role of Women-I, Washington, D.C., March 24-28, 1988).

2. "Methods of Bible Study," approved by the Executive Committee of the General Conference of Seventh-day Adventists at the Annual Council, Rio de Janeiro, Brazil, October 12, 1986, http://www.adventist.org/en/information/official-statements/documents/article/go/0/methods-of-bible-study/ (accessed March 19, 2015).

3. Ibid.

4. For a detailed discussion of recent methods of biblical interpretation, see Clinton Wahlen, "Hermeneutics and Scripture in the Twenty-First Century" (paper presented at the Lake Union Conference Executive Committee, Berrien Springs, Mich., February 13, 2013), http://ordination.lakeunion.org/assets/95352 (accessed March 19, 2015).

5. Philip H. Towner, *The Letters to Timothy and Titus*, New International Commentary of the New Testament (Grand Rapids, MI: Eerdmans, 2006), 251.

6. Timothy Johnson, *The First and Second Letters to Timothy*, Anchor Bible, vol. 35A (New York, NY: Doubleday, 2001), 136.

7. See "Women's Ordination: Group #1 Review of Position Summary #3," August 21, 2014 (paper commissioned by TOSC but not presented), http://www.adventistarchives.org/women's-ordination-group-1-review-of-position-summary-3.pdf (accessed March 19, 2015).

8. See also the answers to Questions 6 and 7 related to this issue of androcentric language in Chapter 11, "More Questions and Answers," under "Questions About Interpretation."

9. See the list in Appendix 2, "English Bible Translations of 1 Timothy 3:2."

10. Walter Scheidel, "Monogamy and Polygyny," in *A Companion to Families in the Greek and Roman Worlds* (ed. Beryl Rawson; Blackwell Companions to the Ancient World; West Sussex, U.K.: Wiley-Blackwell, 2011), p. 108: "Greco-Roman monogamy may well be the single most important phenomenon of ancient history that has remained widely unrecognized." Note also idem, "Monogamy and polygyny in Greece, Rome, and world history" (June 2008), p. 2, http://www.princeton.edu/~pswpc/pdfs/scheidel/060807.pdf (accessed April 2, 2015): "Greek and Roman men were not allowed to be married to more than one wife at a time and not meant to cohabit with concubines during marriage, and not even rulers were exempt from these norms."

11. See Appendix 3, "Similarities Between 1 Timothy and Titus."

12. Kenneth L. Waters, Sr. "Saved through Childbearing: Virtues as Children in 1 Timothy 2:11-15," *Journal of Biblical Literature*, vol. 123, no. 4 (2004), 730.

13. Rod Thomas, quoted in Trevor Grundy, "Archbishop of Canterbury: Anglicans May Split," *Adventist Review*, http://www.adventistreview.org/world-news/archbishop-of-canterbury-anglicans-may-split (accessed March 23, 2015).

FIVE

MUST WOMEN KEEP SILENT?

A s we have seen, 1 Timothy 3:2 is very clear—that the elder/
minister who oversees the church "must be the husband
of one wife." However, some people say that if we're going
to take this text literally, then, according to Paul's instruction in
1 Corinthians 14:34 ("Let your women keep silent in the churches"), women may not ever communicate audibly during the worship service.

Even with this verse, a plain reading of the text saves us from
such extreme and incorrect interpretations. Let's consider some
important points about this passage of Scripture:

▶ Unlike the Pastoral Epistles of Timothy and Titus, which
were written to ministers serving many different areas,
1 Corinthians was written to a specific church in Corinth.

▶ It was written primarily to address specific issues and
questions that came up in Corinth.

▶ 1 Corinthians 14 addresses the practices of three groups
who were causing significant disruptions in the worship
service at Corinth.

▶ These disruptions were caused *by men as well as women*:

❖ men were speaking in tongues without an interpreter
(vss. 27, 28).

51

- ❖ men were prophesying without waiting until others had finished speaking (vss. 29-33).

- ❖ women "kept asking questions" (*eperōtatōsan*)[1] while people were speaking (vss. 34, 35).

▸ Paul commands *all three groups* (including the men who were being disruptive) to "keep silent"—using a very strong word in Greek (*sigaō*)—a word he doesn't use in 1 Timothy where he instructs women during the worship service to learn quietly (1 Tim. 2:11, 12).

We need to remember that Paul is not talking about a Sabbath School class but explaining how the Christians in Corinth could preserve reverence and decorum in worship, which was obviously a problem.

Can you imagine if today in your church men and women were being as disruptive as they were at the church in Corinth? Of course, they would be told to be silent and stop disrupting the service. It doesn't mean that they must forever remain silent. Rather they—both men and women—should speak in Christian love and orderliness.

You may be wondering, if 1 Corinthians 14 was addressing a specific problem in a specific place, at a specific time, why is this letter preserved for us in the Bible today? It is so that we can learn from their example, and see how God views the importance of authority and order. For example, in vs. 32, we are told that "the spirits of the prophets are subject to the prophets" and the following verse states, "For God is not the author of confusion but of peace, as in all the churches of the saints."

Looking a Bit Deeper

But then what does Paul mean when he writes in 1 Timothy 2:11, 12 that women are "to remain quiet" (vs. 12, ESV) or, as some translations misleadingly have it, "to keep silent" (NRSV)?

Of course, when a translation isn't clear, it's always good to look back at the original language. The word in Greek is *hēsychia*, meaning a "state of quietness, without disturbance." Another form of this Greek word is *hēsychion*, used in 1 Timothy 2:2—"that we may lead a *quiet and peaceable* life. . . ." So, when we look at 1 Timothy 2, it's important to realize that in verses 11 and 12 Paul is not stressing *silence* (as in 1 Cor. 14:34 which uses *sigaō*, "to be silent"), but a positive and proactive effort to seek peace and harmony.

In fact, this idea of harmony (*homonoia*) was so prominent in the major cities of Asia Minor in the first century that it is reflected in their coins. The cities of Ephesus, Smyrna, and Pergamum especially engaged in intense political rivalry to be the most prominent city in the Roman province of Asia. This rivalry, of course, was expensive and had negative results, including large city expenditures on wasteful building projects in order to earn status and privilege from Rome. The *homonoia* coins, which depict friendship and harmony between two cities, seem to have been an effort to defuse some of this rivalry.[2]

Plutarch (A.D. 45-120), a Greek historian and author, was well aware of the political climate among the Greek cities. He urged statesmen to act wisely by encouraging their citizens to secure "a life of harmony and quiet" (*meth' hēsychias kai homonoias katabiōnai*), using the same Greek word that is used twice in 1 Timothy 2:11, 12. Might not Paul be expressing here to Timothy a similar thought as a way to avoid rivalry in the churches between men and women?

View of Early Adventists

Certainly early Adventists did not see these scriptures as prohibiting women from speaking in church. Daniel T. Bourdeau, an Adventist minister, missionary, and writer, answered a reader's question about these texts. In *The Advent Review and Sabbath Herald*, Dec. 2, 1862, p. 6, he wrote:

> Paul does not suffer [allow] a woman to teach, or to usurp authority over the man; and we do not learn from the Scriptures that women were ever ordained apostles, evangelists, or elders; neither do we believe that they should teach as such. Yet they may act an important part in speaking the truth to others [quoting Phil. 4:3; Rom. 16:3; Acts 18:2, 26, et al.].[3]

Authoritative Teaching in the Church

In 1 Timothy 2:12, the pair of infinitives "to teach" and "to have authority" are linked together in the stipulation "I do not permit" and refer to Paul's prohibition of women exercising an *authoritative* teaching role over a man in the church. Paul grounds this practice not in culture or custom but in the Genesis account of Creation and the Fall (see 1 Tim. 2:13-14). Women are encouraged to be supportive of God's divine order for church leadership. Within this arrangement, women may have many different teaching roles, such as in Sabbath School classes, seminars, preaching, evangelism, etc.

So what is an authoritative teaching role? In short, it refers to each local congregation being overseen by a biblically-qualified elder or minister (1 Tim. 3:2-7), who is responsible to "preach the word" (2 Tim. 4:2) and ensure that "sound doctrine" characterizes all the church's teaching activities (Titus 1:9). The next chapter looks at this subject in detail.

Endnotes:

1. Italicized words in parentheses give the original Greek words being translated.

2. John Paul Lotz, "The *Homonoia* Coins of Asia Minor and Ephesians 1:21," *Tyndale Bulletin*, vol. 50, no. 2 (1999), 180.

3. D. T. Bourdeau, "Spiritual Gifts," *Advent Review and Sabbath Herald*, vol. 21, no. 1 (December 2, 1862), 6, col. 2.

SIX

THE HEADLESS HORSEMAN RIDES AGAIN

In one form or another, the myth of the headless horseman has terrified people for centuries. In Celtic folk tales, an Irish "dullahan" rides a black horse and carries his head under his lower thigh. Whenever the dullahan stops riding, a death occurs. A popular Scottish tale tells of a headless horseman riding a headless horse as they haunt the Isle of Mull.

German legends by the Brothers Grimm describe a headless man in a long gray coat sitting on a gray horse, and of another headless horseman, called "the wild huntsman," who warns hunters not to ride the next day because they will meet with an accident.

In American folklore, the Headless Horseman is a character from the short story, "The Legend of Sleepy Hollow," written by author Washington Irving. Set in the time of the American Revolutionary War, the ghost of this headless soldier rises from the grave each Halloween and goes galloping about looking for his lost head. Recently, this American tale has been resurrected and reframed in a popular international television series called "Sleepy Hollow."

Heads Are Important

The idea of a headless body *is* terrifying. There's something particularly gruesome about a decapitation; the thought of a head severed from a body is one that gives many people a queasy feeling in their stomach. Every *body* needs a head!

Just as a human body needs a head to function properly, so does the Church. That's why we are told in Ephesians 5:23 that "Christ is head of the church; and He is the Savior of the body."

There is no doubt—at least among Seventh-day Adventists—that Christ is the Head of the Church. He founded the Church (Matt. 16:18) and is its "Chief Shepherd," providing a model of leadership for church undershepherds—the ministers and elders of the Church (1 Pet. 5:1-4).

Context Is Important

So there is no question that Christ, not man, is Head of the Church. Let's remember however, that when we accept a text we accept the passage (or context) *in its entirety*. For example, some Christians accept Exodus 20:8, "Remember the Sabbath day, to keep it holy," but then apply it to Sunday and ignore the rest of the passage—"Six days you shall labor, and do all your work; but the seventh day is a Sabbath to the Lord your God . . ." (vss. 9, 10).

Unfortunately, the same selectivity sometimes happens with other passages, such as Ephesians 5:23. While we understand and embrace the fact that Christ is the Head of the Church, let's look at the verse in its context:

Wives, submit to your own husbands, as to the Lord. For the husband is head of the wife, as also Christ is head of the church; and He is the Savior of the body. Therefore, just as the church is subject to Christ, so let the wives be to their own husbands in everything. Husbands, love your wives just as Christ also loved the church and gave Himself for her (Eph. 5:22-25).

What It's Not Saying

First, let's notice what this text is *not* saying. It's not saying that *all* women are to submit to *all* men. Neither is it saying that wives are to be "subservient" or "subjugated" to their husbands. Subservient means to "obey others unquestioningly,"[1] or to be "less important." To be subjugated means to be brought "under domination or control."[2] This idea is completely unbiblical and is definitely *not* what the text is saying.

On the other hand, to "submit" means to "accept," or "yield to,"[3] to "stop trying to fight."[4] The word can also mean "to present or propose to another for review, consideration."[5]

Of course, "to submit" can also refer to a very negative, controlling situation, which unfortunately can (and does) happen when men don't take to heart the context of the verse and remember that they are to "love your wives just as Christ also loved the church and gave Himself for her" (vs. 25).

What Does It Mean?

So what is this passage actually talking about? It's talking about husbands and wives experiencing together a life of mutual love, understanding, and support. It means that wives and husbands should talk together, consult one another, and come to mutual decisions. It means the husband is to be the protector and provider for his wife—just as Christ is for the Church. It also means that if the two should come to an impasse—as does happen sometimes, the biblical way is for the wife to "submit," or to acquiesce to her husband. Interestingly, *acquiesce* comes from the French word, *acquiescer,* which means to be quiet, tranquil, resting. Acquiesce means "to accept, agree, or allow."

By the way, this doesn't mean that the husband should never listen to his wife. We are sure that there are many examples when a husband has followed his wife's advice, and was glad!

Nevertheless, the text is clear: "Therefore, just as the church is subject to Christ, so let the wives be to their own husbands in everything. Husbands, love your wives just as Christ also loved the church and gave Himself for her" (vss. 24, 25). Just as important as wives yielding to their husbands is the admonition for husbands to love their wives as much as Christ loves the church.

While we don't live in a perfect world and human beings often fall short of God's standards, as His people we know that "As the will of man cooperates with the will of God, it becomes omnipotent. Whatever is to be done at His command may be accomplished in His strength. All His biddings are enablings."[6]

The Christian Household and the Household of God

But how does this relate to the Church? Isn't Paul talking about the marital relationship here between husband and wife? Yes. In Ephesians 5 he is referring to a "household"—in this case, husband and wife. However, in 1 Timothy 3:15 Paul talks about another household—the "household of God"—which is made up of godly men, women, and children.

Just as there are biblical rules (or "codes") for how a Christian household should function, there are also biblical codes for how the household of God—that is, His Church—is to function. This is why Paul wrote his important letters to Titus and to Timothy: "I am writing these things to you so that, if I delay, you may know how one ought to behave in the household of God, which is the church of the living God, a pillar and buttress of the truth" (1 Tim. 3:14, 15). And it is in these pastoral letters of 1 and 2 Timothy and Titus, where we find these Church codes spelled out (vs. 15).[7]

"New Headship Theology?"

For centuries, the Christian Church and household codes given in the New Testament have been understood and practiced by many Christian denominations, including the Seventh-day Adventist Church, and only relatively recently within the last century, have these codes come into question.

It is interesting to note that in 2014 the majority of the General Conference Theology of Ordination Study Committee members found clear evidence in Scripture for a biblical model of male spiritual leadership "that has validity across time and culture."[8]

Sadly, in spite of this, some people refer to "Headship Theology" in a derogatory manner, characterizing as misguided those who take seriously Paul's instructions regarding the home (Eph. 5:22-25) and the church (1 Tim. 2 and 3; Titus 1:5-9). They assert that the idea of male spiritual leadership in the church is a fairly recent teaching (from the 1970s and 1980s) that a few Adventists have tried to bring into the Church.

But history proves otherwise. Let's look at what some well-respected early Adventists wrote.

Male Spiritual Leadership Taught by Early Adventists

In an article titled, "Woman's Place in the Gospel," J. H. Waggoner, editor of *The Signs of the Times*, wrote:

> The divine arrangement, *even from the beginning*, is this, that the man is the head of the woman. Every relation is disregarded or abused in this lawless age. But the Scriptures always maintain this order in the family relation. "For the husband is the head of the wife, even as Christ is the head of the church." Eph. 5:23. Man is entitled to certain privileges which are not given to woman; and he is subjected to some duties and burdens from which the women are exempt. A woman may pray, prophesy, exhort, and comfort the church, *but she cannot occupy the position of a pastor or a ruling elder*. This would be looked on as usurping authority over the men which is here [1 Tim. 2:12] prohibited.[9]

Another clear statement was made by G. C. Tenney, editor of the *Bible Echo*, an Adventist publication in Australia. In his article, "Woman's Relation to the Cause of Christ," published March 15, 1892 in the *Bible Echo* and republished May 24, 1892 in the *Review and Herald*, he wrote:

> Reverting to the teachings of Paul [1 Cor. 14:34-37], whose writings are in question, we discover very clearly that he was the friend, not the adversary, of women in the work of the Christian church. It is true he insists upon God's order being preserved.[10]

Then he went on to explain what that order is, namely, that it is not God's plan for women to run either the home or the Church.

A New Theology?

As we can see, male spiritual leadership in the home and in the Church is not a new idea that arose only in the late twentieth century. Male headship was not even a new idea in the time of the apostle Paul, as indicated by Paul himself in 1 Timothy 2:12, 13, where he refers to God's pre-Fall creation order as supporting his point that men should be the spiritual leaders in God's Church.[11]

Unfortunately, today some Adventists attempt to sweep away any notion of biblical headship by stating that these so-called "headship theology" proponents found "a new way of interpreting the Creation story in which Adam and Eve were equal but not equal," and used this "'principle' that served as a guide for how every Bible text regarding women was to be interpreted."[12]

This is simply not true. First, we have seen that the teaching of male spiritual headship is not new. Second, as Seventh-day Adventists, we dig deeply into Scripture, comparing text with text, building a theology from the entire Bible.

What Does the Bible Say?

Genesis 1 describes the creation of the first human beings in these words: "God created man in His own image, in the image of God He created him; male and female He created them" (Gen. 1:27).

Since both man and woman are created in God's image, both have equal value. Modern culture wants us to think that equal means identical. But equality does not destroy our uniqueness. God believes in diversity, not uniformity. He did not create two Adams—He created an Adam and an Eve—complements to each other as they each filled their God-given roles.

And It Was Very Good

After Adam and Eve were created, "God saw everything that He had made, and indeed it was very good" (Gen. 1:31). In fact, it was perfect. As we gaze into this perfectly created world, we can learn a lot regarding the roles God gave to His crowning acts of creation—man and woman. Let's notice the following from the text:

1. *Order of Creation.* According to Genesis 2, God formed the man (*ha 'adam*)[13] first and placed him in the Garden of Eden to care for it. Before creating Eve, God gave the man instructions about the Tree of the Knowledge of Good and Evil. God brought the animals to him and entrusted him with the responsibility of naming them. When God brought the first female human being to the man, he was also entrusted with naming her. And now for the first time, we hear a human voice in Scripture—it is the man's voice, speaking in beautiful poetry, and calling her "Woman [*'isha*], because she was taken out of man [*'ish*]" (vs. 23):

> *This is now bone of my bones*
>
> *And flesh of my flesh;*
>
> *She shall be called Woman,*
>
> *Because she was taken out of Man.*

The parallelism of these two naming accounts, using the same Hebrew verb (*qara'*) for "he called/named," is another indication showing that the man is given the primary leadership role in this new world, which is why Adam was created before Eve.

Some opponents argue, following this reasoning, that the animals would have dominance over Adam since they were created before man. However this argument supports the evolutionary theory that humans are just part of the animal kingdom, without acknowledging that human beings were made "in the image of God" and were to "have dominion" (Gen. 1:16) over the animals and other living creatures. Notice that the text does not say that Adam was to "have dominion" over Eve.

2. *The man takes primary responsibility.* Another indication that Adam was made the primary leader is found in Genesis 2:24: "Therefore a man shall leave his father and mother and be joined [literally, "cling"] to his wife, and they shall become one flesh." It isn't simply coincidence that the man is told to take the initiative in leaving his father and mother (notice again the order: male, then

female). The reason given for the man to leave his parents is that he might "cling" or "hold onto" his wife. This suggests that he is to take responsibility for their staying together and for her protection. So Adam is created as the prototypical man (Gen. 2:7, 15-23) as well as the representative husband (2:24, 25).

3. *A different role given to woman from the beginning.* The role of the woman in the Creation story in Genesis 2 is different from Adam, though no less important. To begin with, she was "built" (*banah*) from one of the man's ribs. God could have made the woman from the dust of the ground (as he did for man), in order to show that they were exactly the same, but the Creator's interactions with the man before the woman's creation and the way in which she was created indicate a difference in function.

The fact of the woman being created from the man's side shows both woman's equality to man and identity to him in terms of nature; yet it also underscores that man was created first and was given by God the primary responsibility for leadership of the human family. The woman is designated by God as "a helper comparable to him [man]" (Gen. 2:18).

A Helper Comparable to Him

The Hebrew term here (*'ezer*), in both its noun ("helper") and verb ("help") forms most commonly refers to divine help, (such as in Gen. 49:25, Deut. 33:26, and Ps. 115:9-11), but it can also refer to help given by human beings. For example, God warned the prince of Jerusalem that he would scatter all his *helpers* and troops (Ezek. 12:14), a clear example where the noun refers to human beings. The verb is used in a similar way: the two and a half tribes *helped* the larger segment of Israel to conquer Canaan (Josh. 1:14; similarly, 10:6); Abishai *helped* David against the Philistines (2 Sam. 21:17); armed forces from Manasseh came to *help* David shortly before Saul's death (1 Chr. 12:19-21 [Hebrew, vss. 20-22]); troops provided *help* to King Uzziah against the enemy (2 Chr. 26:13); and valiant men *helped* King Hezekiah cut off the water supply outside Jerusalem in advance of Sennacherib's attack (2 Chr. 32:3).

Since the word itself (*'ezer*) says nothing about the relative status of the one giving help, that must be decided by context. But notice that, in all of these examples of *'ezer* being a term for human help, the status of the one being helped is greater: the larger portion of Israel is helped by the smaller segment and kings of Israel receive the help. This usage also fits the Genesis creation account—the man has the leading role while the woman is created "for him" (*lo*) as a supportive helper (*'ezer*).

Equality of Personhood

Paul understands this perspective when he cites Genesis 1 and 2 in supporting different roles in the Church for men and women within the framework of equality of personhood (see 1 Cor. 11:7-9 and 1 Tim. 2:13).

It's important to remember that the Creation order of the woman being created from the man does not in any way suggest superiority or inferiority to him or a domineering/subservient relationship, nor does it suggest a male-female caste system. Ellen White wrote that "Eve was created from a rib taken from the side of Adam, signifying that she was not to control him as the head, nor to be trampled under his feet as an inferior, but to stand by his side as an equal, to be loved and protected by him."[14]

Harmonious Relationship Attacked

Unfortunately, the happy, harmonious relationship in Eden of two equals— both trusting in God as their Father, one as leader and the other as supportive helper—soon comes under attack. In telling the sad history of the Fall, Genesis 3 describes the overthrow of God's Creation order: the man is absent; the serpent talks to the woman as if she were the head and representative of the family; and the woman accepts the role given to her by the serpent. In fact, the serpent goes further, claiming that God's prohibition "was given to keep them [Adam and Eve] in such a state of subordination that they should not obtain knowledge, which was power."[15] Eve's reply to the insinuation of unfairness, with its slight but telling variation on God's actual command, reflects already the evil influence of the serpent in its selfish characterization of God: "We may eat the fruit of the trees of the garden; but of the fruit of the tree which is in the midst of the garden, God has said, 'You shall not eat it, *nor shall you touch it,* lest you die'" (Gen. 3:2, 3).

The man's activity and initiative had been the focus in Genesis 2, but now in chapter 3 the woman is shown taking the initiative. Based on her conversation with the serpent, she *reasons* to a decision, *takes* of the forbidden fruit, *eats* it, and *gives* some of it to Adam (vs. 6).

Total Leadership Reversal

In sharp contrast with Genesis 2, in which the woman is called "his woman" or "wife" (vs. 24) the man is now called "her man" or "husband" (3:6). In short, there is a total reversal of leadership based on the Creation order. The man ate the fruit second, following the initiative and example of the woman. Paul points to the roles of men and women established at Creation and the consequences of its reversal as a scriptural basis for preserving male teaching authority in the Church (1 Tim. 2:13, 14).

Man's Decisive Act

The dramatic significance of this reversal is highlighted by the way Genesis describes the results of the Fall. The man's decision to eat the fruit is the decisive act, not the woman's. How do we know this?

1. Only after Adam eats did the negative consequences become clear: the eyes of both were opened; they knew they were naked and sewed fig leaves into loincloths; then they heard God coming and hid themselves (Gen. 3:7, 8).

2. When God confronts this challenge to His command, he seeks out Adam, not Eve, as the one to be held principally responsible: "the LORD God called to the man and said to him, "Where are you?" The pronoun *you* in Hebrew is a masculine singular form, referring only to Adam.

3. In questioning the pair, it is clear that the man bears the pri-

mary responsibility. God first questions Adam at length, and only afterward questions the woman briefly (see Gen. 3:9-11).

4. In pronouncing judgment upon Adam, God emphasizes the man's surrender of his leadership responsibility as the first misstep even before eating the fruit: "Because you have listened to the voice of your wife and have eaten of the tree . . . ." (vs. 17).

In recognition of God's headship principle, Paul assigns full responsibility for the Fall of the human race to Adam, as indicated in 1 Corinthians 15:22: "For as in Adam all die, even so in Christ all shall be made alive" (see also Rom. 5:12-19).

Consequences of Sin

The Fall injects sin into the world, bringing pain and suffering into all human experience. Existing relationships are changed. Adam no longer wants to identify with Eve, going out of his way to avoid calling her "my wife" and instead uses a very long phrase: "the woman whom You gave to be with me." In doing this, Adam also distances himself from his Creator and places the blame for sin on God, just as Lucifer did in heaven.

After the Fall, there would be a power struggle. God tells Eve that her desire will now be "toward" ('el) her husband (vs. 16). The Hebrew preposition 'el can be translated either positively ("for") or negatively ("against"). When it describes an action "of a hostile character," it should be translated "against."[16] This meaning makes more sense in view of Genesis 4:7, which uses nearly the same wording. In that verse, God warns that sin's desire would be to control Cain, but that he must rule over it. Similarly, in 3:16, God warns Eve that now, because of sin, "your desire will be *against* your husband" (vs. 16).[17] She will want to dominate and control him (as happened already in her urging him to eat the forbidden fruit).[18]

God's remedy for this situation is for Adam's headship to continue: "he shall rule over you" (vs. 16). Whether man's headship role would be predominantly positive or negative would depend on whether he would exercise this role with God's loving headship in view (as outlined in Eph. 5:25), as well as on the woman's willingness to accept it. Unfortunately, as Ellen White observes, "man's abuse of the supremacy thus given him has too often rendered the lot of woman very bitter and made her life a burden."[19]

Before sin, the relationship of the man and woman was perfect and harmonious, with Adam exercising unselfish leadership and Eve providing help and encouragement.

Theory and Practice

I (Gina) must admit that this discussion about headship can sound pretty theoretical—until you put it into practice. For example, there was a time when I completely ignored the idea of submission, as outlined in Ephesians 5. After maturing in my spiritual walk, I no longer ignored the text, but still struggled with its meaning. Finally, one day I decided to have a frank talk with God about it.

"God," I prayed. "I believe that the Bible—all of it—is Your Word, and that includes Ephesians 5. But do You really mean that I should submit to my husband? And what does it mean to 'submit' to him? I really want to understand this text—will you please show me the real meaning?"

Peace enfolded me like a warm blanket. I knew that God had heard my sincere plea and that He would answer. But I was amazed at how clearly and quickly he answered my prayer.

My husband had enrolled us in supplemental health insurance for cancer coverage. I thought it wasn't a bad idea until I saw how much was coming out of our paychecks each month for this extra coverage.

"I don't think we need this cancer insurance after all," I told Clint. "Look at how much we're paying for it! Besides, what are the chances of you or I getting cancer? We're both in good health." Even our tax man agreed—we should cancel this unnecessary expense.

"But I really think we should keep this coverage," Clint persisted. "What would we do *if* one of us was diagnosed with cancer? Treatment is very expensive and our regular insurance doesn't cover everything. We could still end up owing thousands of dollars."

I still wasn't convinced—all I could see were the monthly deductions from the paycheck.

But then I remembered, "Wives, submit to your own husbands, as to the Lord. For the husband is head of the wife, as also Christ is head of the church; and He is the Savior of the body. Therefore, just as the church is subject to Christ, so let the wives be to their own husbands in everything. Husbands, love your wives just as Christ also loved the church and gave Himself for her (Eph. 5:22-25).

"Well," I told Clint, "I still don't think it's necessary, but if you really believe that it's best to keep the supplemental insurance, then let's keep it."

One month later I was diagnosed with cancer. I had numerous doctor appointments, lab tests, major surgery, and radiation treatment. Through it all the costs were completely covered by insurance, all because I decided to follow the Bible and do what it says. Today, praise God, I am cancer-free.

Similar blessings flow from following God's leadership plan for the Church.

Endnotes:

1. Urban Dictionary, http://www.urbandictionary.com/define.php?term=subservient (accessed March 23, 2015).

2. *Concise Oxford English Dictionary*, 12th ed. (New York, Oxford University Press, 2011), 1436.

3. Ibid.

4. Merriam-Webster Online Dictionary, http://www.merriam-webster.com/dictionary/submit (accessed March 23, 2015).

5. Ibid.

6. Ellen G. White, *Christ's Object Lessons* (Washington, D.C.: Review and Herald, 1941), 333.

7. For more information on household and church codes, see Clinton Wahlen, "Is 'Husband of One Wife' in 1 Timothy 3:2 Gender-Specific?" (paper presented at the Theology of Ordination Study Committee, Columbia, MD, January 23, 2014), 21, 22, https://www.adventistarchives.org/is-"husband-of-one-1-wife"-in-1-timothy-32-gender-specific.pdf (accessed March 18, 2015).

8. *Theology of Ordination Study Committee Report*, 100, www.adventistarchives.org/final-tosc-report.pdf (accessed March 18, 2015).

9. J. H. Waggoner, "Woman's Place in the Gospel," *The Signs of the Times*, Dec. 19, 1878, 380, col. 3 (emphasis supplied).

10. G. C. Tenney, "Woman's Relation to the Cause of Christ," *The Advent Review and Sabbath Herald*, May 24, 1892, 329, col. 1.

11. For a more detailed discussion, see Chapter 5, "Must Women Keep Silent in Church?"

12. Martin Hanna and Cindy Tutsch, eds., *Questions and Answers About Women's Ordination* (Nampa, ID: Pacific Press, 2014), 150.

13. Italicized words in parentheses give the original Hebrew text being translated.

14. Ellen G. White, *Patriarchs and Prophets* (Mountain View, CA: Pacific Press, 1958), 46.

15. Ellen G. White, *Confrontation* (Washington, D.C.: Review and Herald, 1971),13, 14.

16. Francis Brown, S. R. Driver, and Charles A. Briggs, *A Hebrew and English Lexicon of the Old Testament* (Oxford: Oxford University Press, 1907), 40 (§413.4).

17. Cf. the New English Translation: "You will want to control your husband" (Gen. 3:16, NET).

18. Commenting on Genesis 3:16, Derek Kidner, *Genesis: An Introduction and Commentary*, Tyndale New Testament Commentary, vol. 1 (Downers Grove, IL: InterVarsity, 1967), 71, describes the changed relation this way: "'To love and to cherish' becomes 'To desire and to dominate.'"

19. White, *Patriarchs and Prophets*, 58.

SEVEN

BUT WHAT ABOUT ELLEN WHITE?

"Ellen White was ordained," a friend told me not long ago. "And I can prove it—I have a copy of her ordination certificate."

Having been a tour guide for six years at "Elmshaven," Ellen G. White's last home, located in St. Helena, California, I (Gina) was familiar with the subject of the "ordination certificate."

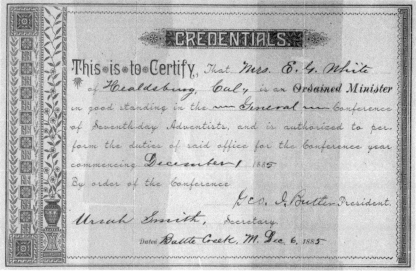

When visitors first enter Elmshaven, they are directed into a main-level room with a fireplace that had at one time been the bedroom of Sara McEnterfer, Ellen White's assistant and traveling companion. Today the room contains many historical objects and papers neatly on display in glass cases. On the top shelf of one of these display cases is a copy of a ministerial credential certificate issued by the General Conference for Mrs. E. G. White—with the word *Ordained* neatly crossed out. The certificate was signed by then G. C. President George I. Butler and Uriah Smith, G. C. secretary, at Battle Creek, Michigan on December 6, 1885.

The original copy of these credentials, which is housed at the White Estate in Silver Spring, Maryland, is one of at least six such certificates, some of which do not have the word *Ordained* crossed out. So was she, or was she not, ordained?[1]

Was Ellen White Ordained?

Ellen White referred twice to God's call for her to serve as "the Lord's messenger."[2] The first statement was made in 1906:

At the age of 78 I am still toiling. We are all in the hands of the Lord. I trust in Him; for I know that He will never leave nor forsake those who put their trust in Him. I have committed myself to His keeping.

And I thank Christ Jesus our Lord, who hath enabled me, for that He counted me faithful, putting me into the ministry.[3]

Five years later, looking back to the very beginning of her prophetic ministry, she wrote: "In the city of Portland [Maine] the Lord ordained me as His messenger, and here my first labors were given to the cause of present truth."[4]

Clearly, in this sense, Ellen White was ordained. However, this ordination was a very special one from the Lord Himself to be His prophet. This sets it apart from all other forms of ordination.

According to the Trustees of the Ellen G. White Estate, Ellen White "was never ordained by human hands, nor did she ever perform a wedding, organize a church, or conduct a baptism."[5]

Yet from 1871 until her death she was granted the same ministerial credentials held by ordained ministers. On the certificate dated 1885, the word *Ordained* is neatly struck out, but on the next one we have from 1887, it isn't. Because of this, some people suggest that Ellen White must have been ordained between 1885 and 1887. However, if that is the case, why had she been voted the credentials of an ordained minister for the previous fifteen years?[6] In fact, on the first of the surviving certificates, dated October 1, 1883, the word *Ordained* has not been struck out. No one would argue that the crossing out of *Ordained* in 1885 meant that she had somehow been "un-ordained" in that year.

Instead, the crossing out of *Ordained* shows the awkwardness of giving credentials to a prophet—an office for which the Church obviously has no special credential. So the Church of that time issued to Ellen White the highest credentials it could. Yet the prophet really needed no human credentials. Hers was an even higher calling, ordained by God Himself, as shown by the fact that before 1871 she served as "the Lord's messenger" for more than twenty-five years without any credentials.

Ellen White Answers the Question

Besides this, Ellen White herself clearly indicates that she was not an ordained minister. On her "Biographical Information Sheet" filled out in 1909 for the General Conference records, the question is asked, "If ordained, state when, where, and by whom." Beside this question (Item 19 on the form), we simply find an "X"— the same response she gave to Item 26, which asks, "If remarried, give date, and to whom."

Marking these two separate questions with an "X" indicates that Ellen White never remarried, nor had she ever been ordained. She is not here denying that God had called and gifted her for a unique prophetic ministry; she is simply responding to the obvious intent of the question, indicating that no ordination ceremony had ever been carried out for her.[7] As she indicated in 1903, "No one has ever heard me claim the position of leader of the denomination."[8]

Ellen White and Women's Ordination

The closest that Ellen White came to calling for women to be ordained is in the following statement, published in 1895:

Women who are willing to consecrate some of their time to the service of the Lord should be appointed to visit the sick, look after the young, and minister to the necessities of the poor. They should be set apart to this work by prayer and laying on of hands. In some cases they will need to counsel with the church officers or the minister, but if they are devoted women, maintaining a vital connection with God, they will be a power for good in the church. This is another means of strengthening and building up the church. We need to branch out more in our methods of labor. Not a hand should be bound, not a soul discouraged, not a voice should be hushed; let every individual labor, privately or publicly, to help forward this grand work. Place the burdens upon men and women of the church, that they may grow by reason of the exercise, and thus become effective agents in the hand of the Lord for the enlightenment of those who sit in darkness.[9]

This statement clearly calls for the setting apart of women to a special work "by prayer and laying on of hands." Some have even described this as calling for some kind of "ordination," although Ellen White does not use the word here.

What is this special work to which women should be set apart? Let's allow Ellen White herself to define what she means:

1. This ministry is part-time. "Women who can devote *some of their time* . . . ." So right from the start, she doesn't seem to be referring to pastoral ministry. In fact, in the first half of the article she has already dealt with that, indicating that *all* "lay" members of the church, both men and women,[10] have a part in spreading the gospel:

Ministers should take the officers and members of the church into their confidence, and teach them how to labor for the Master. Thus the minister will not have to perform all the labor himself, and at the same time the church will receive greater benefit than if he endeavored to do all the work, and release the members of the church from acting the part which the Lord designed that they should.[11]

2. The work is something other than what the church was already doing. The church already had full-time gospel ministers. "This is *another means* of strengthening and building up the church. We need to branch out more in our methods of labor."

3. It may not even involve holding a church office in the usual sense of the term. The women "should be *appointed* to visit the sick, look after the young, and minister to the necessities of the poor." The statement itself makes clear that this work is not equated with that of a minister, or even church officers such as the elder, who was responsible to lead the congregation, because it goes on to say that sometimes these women "will need to counsel *with the church officers or minister.*"

What Kind of Ministry?

So was Ellen White here calling for ordaining women to ministry? Only if we think of ministry in the broadest possible sense. On the other hand, she has clearly distinguished this ministry from that of the pastor and the leading church officers. To claim that this statement supports ordaining women to positions of congregational leadership or full-time gospel ministry is simply not supported by the content of the statement itself.

The emphasis of the article from which this often-quoted statement comes is quite different, as a candid reading of the entire article makes clear. Let's notice another quotation from the same article, which even specifies one of the duties of these women, who, by the way, are described as *helpers* to the minister:

Let all press forward, shoulder to shoulder. Is not every true follower of Christ open to receive his teachings? And should not all have an opportunity to learn of Christ's methods by practical experience? Why not put them to work visiting the sick and assisting in other ways, and thus keep the church in a workable condition? All would thus be kept in close touch with the minister's plans, so that he could call for their assistance at any moment, and they would be able to labor intelligently with him. All should be laborers together with God, and then the minister can feel that he has helpers in whom it is safe to trust. The minister can hasten this desirable end by showing that he *has* confidence in the workers by setting them to work.[12]

Were Physicians Ordained as Ministers?

Since Ellen White said that women should train as physicians and, in another statement, that physicians engaged in missionary work and soul-winning are to be *set apart*, some have suggested that Ellen White is here authorizing the ordination of women:

> The work of the true medical missionary is largely a spiritual work. It includes prayer and the laying on of hands; he therefore should be as sacredly set apart for his work as is the minister of the gospel. Those who are selected to act the part of missionary physicians, are to be set apart as such. This will strengthen them against the temptation to withdraw from the sanitarium work to engage in private practice. No selfish motive should be allowed to draw the worker from his post of duty. We are living in a time of solemn responsibilities; a time when consecrated work is to be done. Let us seek the Lord diligently and understandingly.[13]

If Ellen White had intended that some physicians be ordained *as ministers* she could have said it much more directly, that the true medical missionary "should be set apart *as a minister*." Instead, she writes that he is to be *as sacredly set apart* as is the minister. The missionary physician is to be "set apart as such," meaning as a *missionary physician*. She even explains the motivation for doing this—to strengthen physicians against the temptation to leave the sanitarium (hospital) work to engage in private practice.

What might our medical work look like today if we had such a team of missionary physicians, devoting their entire life to a medical ministry modeled after the ministry of Jesus in meeting people's needs, winning their confidence, and ultimately inviting them to follow Him?[14] Enlisting physicians as ministers would not likely accomplish that, but setting them apart as missionary physicians might.

As we read Ellen White's statement, we don't need to guess what kind of work she intended these medical missionaries to do. In speaking of the spiritual nature of their work, she wrote that it "involves prayer and the laying on of hands." No one would argue that this means medical missionaries should be ordaining people to the gospel ministry, or even ordaining elders. Clearly, she is referring here to offering prayer for the sick.[15] This statement shows that her expression "prayer and the laying on of hands" may refer to something other than ordination to the gospel ministry.

Women Licensed to Preach

Not long after regularizing the credentialing of ordained ministers in 1861 by the Michigan Conference and organizing the General Conference in 1863, the system of issuing licenses to individuals who seemed to be promising candidates for ministry began. The purpose of these licenses was to authorize as workers those sensing a call to ministry so that they might "prove their calling by active work in the cause of God"[16] and "improve their gift in preaching as the way may open."[17]

The first woman to receive a license to preach was Sarah A. (Hallock) Lindsay in September of 1869.[18] Working effectively alongside her husband, she multiplied their effectiveness across a large area of New York and Pennsylvania. From that time on and into the 1900s the Adventist Church issued such licenses to both women and men. We should keep in mind that in this early period, there were very few ministers and no established path to ordination. Therefore, the fact that licenses were granted to women is not an indication that the Church eventually intended to ordain them. The policy calling for an examination prior to licensing anyone came only in 1878, nearly ten years after the first woman licentiate.

In fact, in the beginning of the Advent movement ordained ministers were simply called the "preaching brethren." Later, once the Church began issuing licenses to preach, those who were ordained were called "ministers" and given "credentials," while the others were called "licentiates" and were issued "licenses."[19] For most of Adventist Church history, this was a highly significant distinction—as one seasoned administrator explained in 1942:

The licensed minister does not have authority to preside at any of the church ordinances. He cannot administer baptism or the Lord's Supper, or perform the marriage ceremony. He cannot preside at sessions or meetings of the church in which members are received into fellowship or dismissed from church membership. His ministerial license does not clothe him with such authority. He is authorized to preach, to assist in a spiritual way in any church activities, to lead out in missionary work, and especially to engage in evangelistic efforts.[20]

With this distinction between ministers and licentiates in mind, it is highly significant that Ellen White *never* calls for women to be "ministers." Substitution of the term *pastors* for *ministers* is a relatively recent phenomenon. It wasn't until after World War II that Adventist ministers in large numbers became "settled pastors" assigned to specific churches.[21] Wisely, our pioneers had deliberately resisted this concept of ministry so prevalent in other denominations then and now.[22] Here also, they looked to the Bible for guidance, as James White explains:

It does not appear to have been the design of Christ that his ministers should become stationed, salaried preachers. Of his first ministers it is said, immediately after receiving their high commission, that "they went forth, and preached everywhere, the Lord working with them, and confirming the word with signs following." Mark xvi, 15–20. . . .

Paul was not what is now called a "settled pastor," yet at Corinth "he continued a year and six months, teaching the word of God among them." [Acts 18:11]. These early teachers of Christianity remained in one city, or place, till their testimony aroused the people, and they had brought out a body of believers, and established them in the doctrine of Christ. Things were then set in order so that these disciples could sustain the worship of God. And then these ministers would pass on to a new field of labor. These churches were not carried upon the shoulders of their ministers, but were left to sustain the worship of God among themselves. Occasionally would they pass through and visit the brethren, to exhort, confirm, and comfort them.[23]

Obviously, since those receiving a license were expected to travel widely rather than to remain in one place, most of the women, such as Sarah Lindsay, were wives of ordained ministers, though some unmarried women received licenses too.[24] Generally, these women were not appointed to serve as leaders of churches.[25] Some were, however, gifted public speakers and evangelists.[26] As we will see in the next chapter, such women were engaged in the very work that Ellen White was encouraging women to do. It was not until twelve years after the first woman was licensed that the question of whether or not women should be ordained came up for consideration.

The 1881 Resolution to Ordain Women

At the 1881 General Conference session, two resolutions dealing with ordination were presented for consideration, one more general dealing with the spiritual fitness of ministerial candidates and the second addressing the ordination of women. The first resolution reads:

Resolved, That all candidates for license and ordination should be examined with reference to their intellectual and spiritual fitness for the successful discharge of the duties which will devolve upon them as licentiates and ordained ministers.[27]

The Spiritual Fitness of Ministers

This resolution, which was voted on and adopted, expanded the 1878 mandate for examining candidates for license to include candidates for ordination. However, it did something else that was perhaps even more significant. The 1878 action had specified only that candidates for license be examined "in regard to their doctrinal and educational qualifications."[28] This new resolution stipulated "That all candidates for license and ordination should be examined with reference to their *intellectual and spiritual fitness*."[29] There is a clear shift in emphasis. At least as important, and perhaps even more important than doctrinal knowledge and amount of education, is the spirituality of the ministerial candidate, an emphasis that is in line with the expressed biblical qualifications in 1 Timothy 3 and Titus 1.

This resolution also echoed Ellen White's concerns about the prevailing conditions among ministers of the Church at that time—conditions that led her to call for reform. In a testimony published the year before the General Conference adopted this resolution, she made an explicit call for a change in the examination of ministerial candidates' qualifications: "There must be a decided change in the ministry. A more critical examination is necessary in respect to the qualifications of a minister."[30]

She made it clear that the problem was spiritual: "The ministry is corrupted by unsanctified ministers. Unless there shall be altogether a higher and more spiritual standard for the ministry, the truth of the gospel will become more and more powerless."[31] In view of this call for spiritual qualifications to be put in place, this 1881 resolution—revising the criteria to examine a person's "spiritual fitness" before granting a license or credential as a minister—seems to be a clear response to this call.

Resolution on Women's Ordination

The second resolution considered by the 1881 General Conference addressed the ordination of women:

Resolved, That females possessing the necessary qualifications to fill that position, may, with perfect propriety, be set apart by ordination to the work of the Christian ministry.[32]

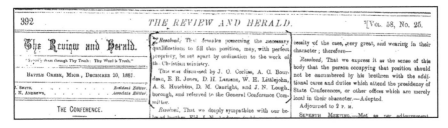

Some have suggested that this resolution was voted on and then given to the General Conference Committee to implement. This is not correct or else the record would have made that clear. The first resolution calling for spiritual qualifications for church ministry, was voted on and "adopted," whereas this one on ordaining women was "referred to the General Conference Committee."[33] Were the three men who composed this committee obstinately thwarting the will of the church in 1881 because this resolution was never brought back for consideration? If this was the case, we might expect that someone would bring the subject up again at the General Conference session in 1882, or in 1883, or in 1884. In fact, General Conference sessions were held yearly until 1889, when they started meeting every two years, but the resolution was never reintroduced.

Some may think that the matter was referred to the GC Committee because the proposal needed more work, or perhaps some rewording. However, this is not the case. In studying this issue and how such resolutions were handled in the nineteenth century, David Trim, director of the Office of Archives, Statistics, and Research of the General Conference, concluded: "Referring resolutions from the Resolutions Committee to the GC Committee was a tactful way of rejecting them."[34] In short, the committee never returned it to the General Conference session because it was never expected to.

Unlike today's situation, the issue of women's ordination in the late nineteenth century apparently created little debate. The minutes of the session record not only the resolutions and their outcome, but the names of those who spoke to them.[35] The first resolution, calling for examining ministers' qualifications, does not seem controversial. Nine people spoke to it, and it was adopted. The next resolution, calling for ordaining women to the ministry, had eight people speak to it, and it was referred to committee. Considering all the facts, including that the measure was never reintroduced, it seems clear that the idea of ordaining women had very little support in the church at that time.

Ellen White's Silence

Ellen White was not present at the 1881 General Conference session. She likely read the report of the resolutions in the *Review* a few weeks later or heard about them from her son Willie, but we have no record of her making any comment one way or the other on the matter.

Of course, we must be careful with arguments from silence, because they can never be proved or disproved. Ellen White's silence *by itself* means little. But if she favored it, why didn't she speak out when the church turned away from ordaining women? On the other hand, if she did not favor ordaining women, some reasons for her silence readily suggest themselves:

1. She may have felt that the issue was simply not that important. Or,

2. If she felt that the church should not ordain women, she may have made no comment on the resolution because none was necessary. The church was not about to begin ordaining women, so no correction was needed.

Silence of Ellen White During a Crisis

Interestingly, we know of another time when the church faced real dangers that Ellen White was warned of in vision, yet she kept silent. In connection with the crisis over pantheism that came to a head with the publication of Dr. John Harvey Kellogg's book *Living Temple*, she wrote the following:

> About the time that *Living Temple* was published, there passed before me in the night season, representations indicating that some danger was approaching, and that I must prepare for it by writing out the things God had revealed to me regarding the foundation principles of our faith. A copy of *Living Temple* was sent me, but it remained in my library, unread. From the light given me by the Lord, I knew that some of the sentiments advocated in the book did not bear the endorsement of God, and that they were a snare that the enemy had prepared for the last days. I thought that this would surely be discerned, and that it would not be necessary for me to say anything about it.[36]

If the church leaders had seen the danger of the concepts in *Living Temple* and moved against it, evidently Ellen White would not have said anything. Yet her silence in regard to pantheism did not mean that it was okay. Only when it was clear that the error was gaining ground did she speak out—and then she did so vigorously.

Ellen White's silence can be just as meaningful as when she spoke out. God's intervention is unnecessary as long as church leaders know their Bibles and follow the guidance of the Holy Spirit. Of course, even sometimes when she did speak out, some did not listen and God's further intervention was necessary. In the case of the book *Living Temple*, fire swept through the Review and Herald publishing house destroying both the plates and unfinished copies of the first edition of the book.[37]

So, when the church considered a resolution in 1881 to ordain women to the ministry and that view did not prevail, the fact that Ellen White said nothing about it should tell us something. If, on the other hand, the church's refusal to ordain women had been an error and that error had triumphed at the General Conference, then we might well expect her to have spoken out against that rejection.

Charged to Protest Injustice

Especially would we expect Ellen White to have spoken out against denying ordination to women if such a denial were arbitrary, unjust, and oppressive. She stated:

> I was charged not to neglect or pass by those who were being wronged. I was specially charged to protest against any arbitrary or overbearing action toward the ministers of the gospel by those having official authority. Disagreeable though the duty may be, I am to reprove the oppressor, and plead for justice. I am to present the necessity of maintaining justice and equity in all our institutions.[38]

Women were given a license to preach and evangelize, but the church officials meeting at this General Conference Session did not see fit to ordain them as ministers. Ellen White spoke strongly

▶ in favor of women workers being paid and paid fairly,

▶ about the importance of supporting aged ministers,[39]

▶ against unfair treatment of black ministers,[40]

but she said nothing when the leaders in 1881 declined to permit licensed women ministers to be ordained.

Even though the instruction to protest unfairness came twenty-five years later, in 1906, the practice of not ordaining women prevailed to the end of Ellen White's life and beyond. Evidently, she didn't see this practice as "arbitrary," "overbearing," or a matter of "justice and equity." She had been "specially charged to protest" against such things, but she didn't protest the practice of not ordaining women. Without seeking to claim too much, her silence on the issue of ordaining women, especially in light of all we have looked at, should make us think very carefully before claiming that her statements of support for women in ministry were somehow meant to nudge the church into ordaining them.

Women as Pastors to the Flock

Another often-quoted statement of Ellen White used to support the idea that women should be ordained as ministers comes from *Testimonies to the Church*, vol. 6: "It is the accompaniment of the Holy Spirit of God that prepares workers, both men and women, to become pastors to the flock of God."[41]

Some argue that this statement calls for women, through the preparation of the Holy Spirit, to become gospel ministers in the commonly accepted sense of the term today—a conference-employed, perhaps even ordained, leader of a local congregation. But although *pastor* may be the commonly used term now for this work, it was not the word Ellen White or the church at that time used. Those "laboring in word and doctrine" she normally called *ministers*, not pastors.[42] So it would be very surprising if that was what Ellen White meant here. In fact, a quick search of her published writings shows that occurrences of *minister* in its various forms (verb forms included), outnumber use of similar words built around *pastor* by more than thirty to one.

Who are "Pastors"?

When we look at how Ellen White actually used the term *pastor,* we find it is often used in connection with *the flock* and showing concern for nurturing God's people, as a shepherd might show tender personal care for each individual sheep. One such instance

where this nurturing connotation is very plain appears in the following account, written from Australia in 1892:

> Elder H used to live here and preach to the people, but he was
> not a shepherd of the flock. He would tell the poor sheep that
> he would rather be horse whipped than visit. He neglected per-
> sonal labor, therefore pastoral work was not done in the church
> and its borders. . . . Had the preacher done the work of a pastor,
> a much larger number would now be rejoicing in the truth.[43]

Let's briefly consider other examples in which Ellen White uses
pastor in a similar way:

Referring to ministers who educated themselves to become debat-
ers, she lamented, "In many respects men trained in this kind of school
unfitted themselves to become pastors of the sheep and lambs."[44]

Speaking of ministers who devoted excessive time to reading and
writing, she indicated that "the duties of a pastor are often shamelessly
neglected because the minister lacks strength to sacrifice his personal
inclinations for seclusion and study. The pastor should visit from house
to house among his flock, teaching, conversing, and praying with each
family, and looking out for the welfare of their souls."[45]

Her concern for personal care of the flock is expressed again this
way:

> Responsibilities must be laid upon the members of the
> church.The missionary spirit should be awakened as nev-
> er before, and workers should be appointed as needed, who
> will act as pastors to the flock, putting forth personal effort to
> bring the church up to that condition where spiritual life and
> activity will be seen in all her borders.[46]

In each of these examples, the *pastor* is to be involved in personal work for the flock of God, even when it is done by "members of the church" rather than the minister. A person—whether
male or female—who visits families, teaching them and praying
with them, showing personal care and interest, is doing pastoral
work. In fact, this was vital, because, as we have seen, Adventist
ministers were not paid to be "settled pastors." They were largely evangelists, sometimes as husband-and-wife teams, raising up

a church in one place, getting it established, and then moving on to another place. In the setting of such an itinerant ministry, when Ellen White spoke of "pastors to the flock of God," she is describing a function more than an office, performed in personal ministry to the sheep of Jesus' flock.

Pastors and Ministers

Looking at the larger context of this statement helps us understand even better this idea of *pastoring* the flock. Let's read this sentence from *Testimonies to the Church*, vol. 6 again, this time *in context* with the entire paragraph:

> All who desire an opportunity for true ministry, and who will give themselves unreservedly to God, will find in the canvassing work opportunities to speak upon many things pertaining to the future, immortal life. The experience thus gained will be of the greatest value to those who are fitting themselves for the ministry. It is the accompaniment of the Holy Spirit of God that prepares workers, both men and women, to become pastors to the flock of God.

The main emphasis is on canvassing—selling books door-to-door. The rest of the paragraph describes the benefits of character and experience that will come to those who engage in the canvassing work. In fact, the title of the entire section of this testimony is: "The Canvasser a Gospel Worker."

Of course, another point emphasized here by Ellen White is that literature evangelism is a good preparation for ministry. It gets the worker out visiting in homes, doing personal labor, seeking to bring the lost sheep into the Lord's flock, that is, *pastoring* the flock of God. It is a work that many can and should do, both men and women, not just ministers.

Personal Ministry in the Home

In a similar passage a few pages later in the same volume, Ellen White clearly shows that her endorsement of canvassing as preparation for the ministry is based on its work of personal ministry in the home:

Some men whom God was calling to the work of the ministry have entered the field as canvassers. I have been instructed that this is an excellent preparation if their object is to disseminate light, to bring the truths of God's word directly to the home circle. In conversation the way will often be opened for them to speak of the religion of the Bible. If the work is entered upon as it should be, families will be visited, the workers will manifest Christian tenderness and love for souls, and great good will be the result. This will be an excellent experience for any who have the ministry in view.

Those who are fitting for the ministry can engage in no other occupation that will give them so large an experience as will the canvassing work.[47]

This personal work in the home, which is at the heart of the canvassing work, is the very method of labor for which Ellen White said women were especially fitted and in which they could do a work "in the line of ministry" that men could not do.[48]

Young Men Are Needed

Elsewhere in this same book Ellen White discusses the need for more ministers to be trained and enter the field. If she had intended to open the regular ministerial option for women, we might well expect her to say so here. But note the references to gender in the following statement:

There is an urgent demand for laborers in the gospel field. *Young men* are needed for this work; God calls for them. Their education is of primary importance in our colleges, and in no case should it be ignored or regarded as a secondary matter. It is entirely wrong for teachers, by suggesting other occupations, to discourage *young men* who might be qualified to do acceptable work in the ministry. Those who present hindrances to prevent *young men* from fitting themselves for this work are counterworking the plans of God, and they will have to give an account of their course. There is among us more than an average of *men* of ability. If their capabilities were brought into use, we should have twenty ministers where we now have one.[49]

This view is reinforced later in the same volume where section seven, "Calls to Service," opens with the article, "Young Men in the Ministry."[50] Among numerous calls in that book for "men" and "young men" to enter the ministry, there is no mention of women being urged to join the ranks of the ministers. If it had been Ellen White's intention earlier in her book to indicate that women as well as men were to prepare for the regular gospel ministry, then we could expect her to mention that here, but she does not.

Such statements of Ellen White are numerous, and many more could be mentioned here. Perhaps it will be sufficient to direct our attention to just a couple more which are typical of the perspective that appears throughout her writings:

> The primary object of our college was to afford *young men* an opportunity to study for the ministry and to prepare *young persons of both sexes* to become workers in the various branches of the cause. . . .

> Those who enter the missionary field should be men and women who walk and talk with God. Those who stand as ministers in the sacred desk should be *men of blameless reputation.*[51]

A clear distinction seems to be made on the basis of gender here, between young men who should "study for the ministry" and young people "of both sexes" to become "workers" in the various branches (or departments) of the Church. Notice too that the second statement, in saying that ministers "should be men of blameless reputation," refers to the qualifications for the elder/minister of 1 Timothy 3:2, where Paul says that the elder "must be blameless, the husband of one wife."

Women Ministers or Pastors?

With this historical background, we are now in a better position to understand Ellen White's statement that "the Holy Spirit . . . prepares workers, both men and women, to become pastors to the flock of God." It seems unlikely that she was calling for women as well as men to be pastors in today's sense of the term. Since she used the term *pastor* to describe a *function* (verb) as well as an *office* (noun) and recognized that the two did not always go together, it's far more likely that, by "pastors to the flock of God," she referred to those exercising a personal ministry of visitation and instruction in the home. If that is indeed her meaning, then it fits with other statements she makes about the kind of work women are especially qualified to do, fulfilling a role that is complementary to that of men. It also harmonizes with her specifically male-directed calls for ministerial workers in the same volume of the *Testimonies*.

If, despite the larger historical setting we have observed for this passage, one continues to insist that it calls for women to serve in the office of *minister*, then why are there no statements that make this point in a clear, straightforward way? On the other hand, as we have seen, there is a work that women are especially qualified to do that men are not. On many occasions, Ellen White described what that work is that women can and should do for the Lord, a topic we turn to in the next chapter.

Endnotes:

1. In this chapter and the following one, we are indebted to William Fagal, associate director of the Ellen G. White Estate, Silver Spring, MD, for permission to adapt material from his paper, "Ellen White and the Role of Women in the Church," revised and submitted to the Biblical Research Institute, December 1987, http://egwtext.whiteestate.org/publication.php?pubtype=Book&bookCode=EWRWC&lang=en&pagenumber=1 (accessed March 19, 2015).

2. On the reason for her use of this self-designation, see Ellen G. White, *Selected Messages. Book One* (Hagerstown, Md.: Review and Herald, 1958), 32.

3. Ellen G. White, *Daughters of God* (Hagerstown, MD: Review and Herald, 2005), 252.

4. Ibid. Originally published in Ellen G. White, "An Appeal to Our Churches Throughout the United States," *The Advent Review and Sabbath Herald*, May 18, 1911, 3, col. 1.

5. The statement appears in Ellen G. White, *Daughters of God*, 249 (Appendix C).

6. In those years, as well as in the years following, her name simply appears in the listings of those being voted ministerial credentials.

7. See the letter from D. E. Robinson to L. E. Froom, quoting W. C. White, in Appendix 4, "Reply on Behalf of W. C. White Regarding Ellen G. White's Credentials." While Mary Steward, one of Ellen White's assistants, actually filled out the form on her behalf, no reason exists to question its accuracy.

8. Ellen G. White, *Testimonies for the Church*, 9 vols. (Mountain View, CA: Pacific Press, 1948), vol. 8, 236.

9. Ellen G. White, "The Duty of the Minister and the People," *The Advent Review and Sabbath Herald*, July 9, 1895, par. 8.

10. "The minister's work is the lay member's work as well" (Ibid., par. 4).

11. Ibid., par. 2.

12. Ibid. (emphasis original).

13. Ellen G. White, *Evangelism* (Washington, D.C.: Review and Herald, 1946), 546 (Ms. 5, 1908).

14. See Ellen G. White, *The Ministry of Healing* (Mountain View, CA: Pacific Press, 1942), 143.

15. This seems to be the medical missionary equivalent of the elders being called upon to pray for and anoint the sick with oil (James 5:14, 15), on which see Ibid., 225-233. Perhaps this is why they are to be as sacredly set apart as the minister/elder.

16. "Business Proceedings of the Eighth Annual Session of the General Conference of S. D. Adventists," *The Advent Review and Sabbath Herald*, March 22, 1870, 110, col. 3.

17. "The Michigan State Conference," *The Advent Review and Sabbath*

Herald, May 26, 1868, 357, col. 1, listing William C. Gage, James G. Sterling, and Uriah Smith as recipients of this license. One year later, licenses were granted for eight others and renewed for these three ("Michigan State Conference," *The Advent Review and Sabbath Herald*, May 25, 1869,173, col. 3).

18. "Report of the N.Y. and Pa. Conference," *The Advent Review and Sabbath Herald*, Oct 12, 1869, 126, col. 3.

19. See, e.g., "The Conference," *The Advent Review and Sabbath Herald*, May 25, 1869, 172, col. 1, which notes that "twenty-two ministers and licentiates were present" at the General Conference held that year. Occasionally, "licensed ministers" could be used for licentiates but "ministers" by itself refers only to ordained ministers.

20. Oliver Montgomery, *Principles of Church Organization and Administration* (Washington, D.C.: Review & Herald, 1942), 134.

21. Ken Corkum, "The Role of the Seventh-day Adventist Minister in Public Evangelism" (D.Min. diss., Andrews University, 1986), 98-101; also 32, 90 for unequivocal statements by A. G. Daniells and George Starr regarding the non-settled nature of ministerial work during Ellen White's lifetime; cf. 50-91 for other related statements by her, Daniells, and others. See also Russell Burrill, *Recovering an Adventist Approach to the Life & Mission of the Local Church* (Fallbrook, CA: Hart, 1998); Idem, *A Study of the Biblical Terms for Clergy and Their Historical Development in Christianity and Adventism* (Berrien Springs, MI: North American Division Evangelism Institute, 1994).

22. See "The Camp-Meeting," La Porte City *Progress*, June 21, 1871, republished in *Advent Review and Sabbath Herald*, June 27, 1871, 12, col. 2: "They have no settled pastors. Their preaching elders are all evangelists, laboring from place to place, under the general supervision of a conference committee of three. Each church has local elders, deacons, and other officers usual to other denominations." Cf. G. I. Butler, "The Systematic-Benevolence Fund and the Ministry," *The Advent Review and Sabbath Herald*, May 6, 1873, 163, col. 1.

23. James White, "'Go Ye Into All the World and Preach the Gospel,'" *The Advent Review and Sabbath Herald*, April 15, 1862, 156, col. 1. In 1902, Ellen G. White, "The Work in Greater New York," *At-*

lantic Union Gleaner, January 8, 1902, 2, reiterated the wisdom of this approach: "There should not be a call to have settled pastors over our churches, but let the life-giving power of the truth impress the individual members to act, leading them to labor interestedly to carry on efficient missionary work in each locality. As the hand of God, the church is to be educated and trained to do effective service. Its members are to be the Lord's devoted Christian workers."

24. E.g., Mrs. S. M. I. Henry, whose husband had died many years earlier from Civil War injuries and who joined the Seventh-day Adventist church late in life. See Chapter 8, "A 'Woman Ministry'"; also Laurel Damsteegt, "S. M. I. Henry: Pioneer in Women's Ministry," *Adventists Affirm* vol. 9, no. 1 (Spring 1995), 17.

25. When men were unavailable or even unwilling to serve in certain areas, some women did serve as leaders of churches, as did, for example, Mabel Vreeland, a credentialed Bible instructor who ministered to churches in upstate New York for a number of years in the mid-twentieth century.

26. E.g., Lulu Wightman and S. M. I. Henry, licensed in 1898, and Minnie Syp (who soon changed the spelling of her surname to Sype), licensed in 1902. Appendix 5, "Women Licensed as Adventist Ministers, 1869-1975," lists the women who received a license to preach, the year they were first licensed, and the conference or organization that issued it.

27. "General Conference: Business Proceedings (Continued)," *The Advent Review and Sabbath Herald*, December 20, 1881, 392, col. 1.

28. "Seventeenth Annual Session of the General Conference of S. D. Adventists," *The Advent Review and Sabbath Herald*, October 17, 1878, 122, col. 1.

29. "General Conference," *The Advent Review and Sabbath Herald*, December 20, 1881, 392, col. 2 (emphasis supplied).

30. White, *Testimonies*, vol. 4, 442.

31. Ibid.

32. "General Conference," *The Advent Review and Sabbath Herald*, December 20, 1881, 392, col. 2.

33. Ibid., cols. 1, 2.

34. David Trim, "The Ordination of Women in Seventh-day Adventist Policy and Practice, up to 1972," revised and slightly expanded version of the paper presented at the Theology of Ordination Study Committee, July 22, 2013, 16, https://www.adventistarchives.org/the-ordination-of-women-in-seventh-day-adventist-policy-and-practice.pdf (accessed March 23, 2015).

35. See "General Conference," *The Advent Review and Sabbath Herald*, December 20, 1881, 392, cols. 1, 2.

36. White, *Selected Messages*, Bk. 1, 202, 203.

37. Arthur L. White, *Ellen G. White*, vol. 5: *The Early Elmshaven Years, 1900-1905* (Washington, D.C.: Review and Herald, 1981), 292.

38. White, *Selected Messages*, Bk. 1, 33 (originally published in *The Advent Review and Sabbath Herald*, July 26, 1906).

39. Ibid.

40. White, *Testimonies*, vol. 9, 223.

41. White, *Testimonies*, vol. 6, 322.

42. See, e.g., Ellen G. White, *Fundamentals of Christian Education* (Nashville, TN: Southern Publishing Association, 1923), 108; Idem, *Gospel Workers* (Hagerstown, MD: Review and Herald, 2005), 76; Idem, *The Publishing Ministry* (Hagerstown, MD: Review and Herald, 1983), 308.

43. Ellen G. White, Document File No. 28A, in *Manuscript Releases*, 21 vols. (Washington, D.C. and Hagerstown, MD: Review and Herald, 1981-1993), vol. 9, 343, 344 ("Experiences in Australia," 53, written in Adelaide, Australia, Oct. 11, 1892).

44. White, Ms. 24, 1888, in *Manuscript Releases*, vol. 12, 196.

45. White, *Gospel Workers*, 337.

46. White, *Testimonies*, vol. 5, 723.

47. White, *Testimonies*, vol. 6, 334.

48. White, Ms. 43a, 1898, in *Manuscript Releases*, vol. 5, 323 (Idem, *Testimonies*, vol. 6, 117).

49. White, *Testimonies*, vol. 6, 135 (emphasis supplied).

50. Ibid., 411-416.

51. White, *Testimonies*, vol. 5, 60, 598 (emphasis supplied).

EIGHT

A "Woman Ministry"

E llen White was clear that "there are women who should labor in the gospel ministry. In many respects they would do more good than the ministers who neglect to visit the flock of God."[1] She added, in connection with fair wages, that "Seventh-day Adventists are not in any way to belittle woman's work."[2]

From statements such as these, some have concluded that Ellen White called for eliminating role distinctions in church ministry between men and women. Since she clearly urged fairness in the treatment and pay of women workers, they infer that this should be understood to include ordination to the gospel ministry without regard to gender. But is that what was intended by these statements? In answering this question, it's helpful to look at the fuller picture.

Women in Ministry

No one exemplified Ellen White's understanding of women in ministry more than S. M. I. [Sarepta Myrenda Irish] Henry. Mrs. Henry was a wife, mother, poet, writer, and national evangelist for the Woman's Christian Temperance Union (WCTU). For most of her life, she was a faithful member of the Methodist Church. After becoming incapacitated by a serious heart condition, she traveled to the Battle Creek Sanitarium in August of 1896. While there, she encountered Christian influences of "sweetness, purity, gentleness," learned of and accepted the seventh-day Sabbath, and was baptized into the Seventh-day Adventist Church.[3] "Mrs. Henry did not parley with specific scriptural truth. She had such a close relationship with Jesus that when she realized the Sabbath's implications for her life she immediately chose to follow Jesus through keeping His day holy."[4]

Despite her weakened condition, she began to share her new-found faith, first with the patients and staff of the sanitarium and then through the pages of the *Review*. Believing that God had touched her spiritual life for some deeper purpose, on April 13, 1897, while joining a group prayer session for the healing of another patient at the sanitarium, Mrs. Henry decided to pray earnestly for her own healing and experienced a miraculous restoration to health.[5] Her healing was medically confirmed by Drs. Kellogg and Kress, who wrote independent accounts of their assessment of her debilitating illness and the remarkable change they observed in the condition of her heart and physical stamina.

Now, as a Seventh-day Adventist, and with Ellen White's encouragement to stay in her role as national evangelist for the WCTU, Mrs. Henry resumed her public speaking (which included camp meetings), wrote articles for the *Review*, answered letters from women writing for help with family and parenting issues, and even drew crowds to attend Adventist evangelistic campaigns. In addition, "those involved with the WCTU now benefited, through Henry's witness, from greater exposure to the light of the Adventist message, which some of them embraced."[6]

One notable occasion at which she lent her influence to public evangelism was in Victoria, British Columbia, a city where it had been very difficult for Adventists to establish a presence. She spoke twice in connection with a series being held there, addressing thousands of people each time and drawing many of them to the evangelistic meetings. This helps us to understand better why Ellen White wrote to her from Australia in 1899, "My sister, there are many ways open before you. Address the crowds whenever you can."

Just what was it that S. M. I. Henry would speak about? The topics of her two presentations in Victoria were "What is the Boy

Worth?" and "Why So Many Children of the Church Go to Ruin."[7] A short time later, while preaching at her son's church in Salt Lake City, amid the towering snow-capped Rockies, she said: "The commonest things are the noblest. Our mountains are awe-inspiring, but the cottage in a cleft is grander and of more importance, because it is the first expression of the will of God. The mountains exist for that little cottage."[8]

She went on to explain how important the cottage, or home, is and that God's hand is over it: "The home is a machine. Its proper work is to turn out men and women to subdue and reclaim a world spoiled by sin. God furnishes the power. God made the home complete—father, mother and child." The care of children has been entrusted by God to fathers and mothers. "The home is a school where God teaches us how to be men and women, how to overcome difficulties, how to solve problems, how to be prepared for the eternal home which He has fitted for His children."[9]

"Address the Crowd Whenever You Can"

The counsel given her by Ellen White to "address the crowd whenever you can" comes from a letter written in 1899 to Mrs. Henry,[10] who had already been granted a ministerial license the previous year.[11] Some have understood this counsel as divine encouragement for women to seek a preaching ministry and to become ordained ministers of the Church. But is that really what Ellen White is promoting here? Not at all, as reference to the immediate context clearly shows. Earlier in the letter, she explains her concern for the women of the Church: "If we can, my sister, we should speak often to our sisters, and *lead* them in the place of saying 'Go.' Lead them to do as we should do: to feel as we should feel, a strong and abiding perception of the value of the human soul. We are learners that we may be teachers. This idea must be imprinted in the mind of every church-member."[12] A little later she again urges, "Teach our sisters that every day the question is to be, Lord, what wilt thou have me to do this day?"

To what work was Ellen White specifically encouraging Mrs. Henry? The first three paragraphs of the letter make it plain:

The work you are doing to help our sisters feel their individual accountability to God is a good and necessary work. Long has it been neglected; but when this work has been laid out in clear lines, simple and definite, we may expect that the essential duties of the home, instead of being neglected, will be done much more intelligently. The Lord would ever have us urge upon those who do not understand, the worth of the human soul.

If we can arrange, as you are now working, to have regularly organized companies intelligently instructed in regard to the part they should act as servants of the Master, our churches will have life and vitality such as have been so long needed.

Christ our Saviour appreciated the excellency of the soul. Our sisters have generally a very hard time, with their increasing families and their unappreciated trials. I have so longed for women who could be educators to help them to arise from their discouragement, and to feel that they could do work for the Lord. And this effort is bringing rays of sunshine into their lives, and is being reflected upon the hearts of others. God will bless you, and all who shall unite with you, in this grand work.[13]

Teaching Ministry

From this letter, it seems that S. M. I. Henry was being encouraged to organize small groups of women in order to instruct them in service for the Lord and that this would add life and vitality to the churches. The *Seventh-day Adventist Encyclopedia* article about her notes:

In 1898 she conceived a plan for what she called "woman ministry." Lecturing on the role of the mother in the moral education of society, she stressed this from coast to coast in the United States and Canada. She also presented her plan to SDA congregations. A. W. Spalding remarked later that in the work instituted in the Seventh-day Adventist Church by Mrs. Henry came "the first semblance of an organized effort to train parents and to give help in their problems."[14]

In light of all this, it seems clear that Ellen White was not encouraging Mrs. Henry to aspire to a pulpit ministry, nor to become a pastor in the usual sense of that term. She was counseling her to continue in her teaching ministry, to use every opportunity that might come her way (including pulpit invitations) to promote her view of "woman ministry" (and, for that matter, lay work irrespective of gender), a view that would strengthen the home and family life and help women see the value and beauty in serving Christ, even within their traditional roles.[15]

"Woman Ministry"

Mrs. Henry's daughter described this woman ministry as being "stupendous in its possibilities." It was a ministry *to women and families by women,* "not," she said, "an organized body of women preachers."[16] S. M. I. Henry herself explained the kind of ministry she had in mind:

> The work of soul-winning can be done most effectually by personal, hand-to-hand effort, in the intercourse of the ordinary home and neighborhood life. A woman's ministry is an especially important one. Our Lord intended that the sweetness of the Gospel should be preached by her; but not necessarily from the platform. If all through the generations she had done her work, it would never have been necessary for her voice to be keyed up to address a public audience.
>
> A woman's holiest ministry is in taking the Gospel to her own children, neighbors and friends, as they come and go about her; talking the words of Christ; pouring out truth in testimony, experience, and consolation. The greatest truths may be served up with the dinner, fitted with a dress pattern, bound in the same bundle with the most common things about which women have been wont to gossip.
>
> The imperative need of our day is that the Christian home shall be indeed a sanctuary and a school, the father and mother united in the ministry of the word of life, and in the teaching of every vital truth; by careful instruction, setting each in its true proportions in its right place in the mind of the growing child;

and that every woman who knows the truth shall find out and love her own work in her own God-appointed place, and become a true minister to all who come within her reach or who can be sought out and helped. And our woman's Gospel work is an effort to help each other to bring all this to pass.[17]

This is remarkably similar to what Ellen White had written just a few years earlier—that first in importance is the proper upbringing of one's own children:

To bring up the children in the nurture and admonition of the Lord is the greatest missionary work that parents can perform. The mother is entrusted with a greater work than is the king upon his throne. She has a class of duty to perform in connection with her children that no other one can perform. If she daily learns in the school of Christ, she will discharge her duty in the fear of God, and care for the children as the Lord's beautiful flock.[18]

Ellen White also urged women to visit door to door and study the Bible with people: "Some women are now teaching young women to work successfully as visitors and Bible readers. Women who work in the cause of God should be given wages proportionate to the time they give to the work."[19] The next few sentences speak of fair wages for ministers' wives who do this work, suggesting that this is the class of women she had principally in view: "As the devoted minister and his wife engage in the work, they should be paid wages proportionate to the wages of two distinct workers, that they may have means to use as they shall see fit in the cause of God. The Lord has put His spirit upon them both." Should the husband die, the wife "is fitted to continue her work in the cause of God, and receive wages for the labor she performs."[20]

Personal Ministry

It would be good for us to allow Ellen White herself to tell us what kind of work she is talking about when she refers to women laboring in the gospel ministry. The counsels just quoted, along with her statement with which this chapter began, opens with the following paragraph:

Some matters have been presented to me in regard to the laborers who are seeking to do all in their power to win souls to Jesus Christ. . . . The ministers are paid for their work, and this is well. And if the Lord gives the wife as well as the husband the burden of labor, and if she devotes her time and her strength to visiting from family to family, opening the Scriptures to them, although the hands of ordination have not been laid upon her, she is accomplishing a work that is in the line of ministry. Should her labors be counted as nought, and her husband's salary be no more than that of the servant of God whose wife does not give herself to the work, but remains at home to care for her family?[21]

The subject under discussion is the pay of ministers' wives, and the kind of work they are doing is described: visiting homes and opening the Scriptures to the families. Further, she dismisses the matter of ordination as irrelevant to the issue, rather than seeing it as a remedy to the injustice regarding pay. Her point is simply that these ministers' wives who labor in this way are "accomplishing a work that is in the line of ministry" and should be paid for it.

Later in the same document she again refers to this visitation-oriented work these women were doing and includes an implied rebuke to the ministers who were not doing it. She writes:

If women do the work that is not the most agreeable to many of those who labor in word and doctrine, and if their works testify that they are accomplishing a work that has been manifestly neglected, should not such labor be looked upon as being as rich in results as the work of the ordained ministers? Should it not command the hire of the laborers?[22]

Context Is Important

It is in this setting that Ellen White's statement, "There are women who should labor in the gospel ministry," appears. The sentence that follows it again underscores the nature of the work she envisioned for these women: "In many respects they would do more good than the ministers who neglect to visit the flock of God." Immediately, she adds, "Husband and wife may unite in this work, and when it is possible, they should. The way is open for consecrated women."[23]

So Ellen White isn't calling for women to have role-interchange-ability with men, but rather a complementary ministry that focuses on personal work. Her statements seem primarily to deal with ministers' wives, encouraging a husband-wife ministry team. She noted the lack of ordination for the woman, but gave no indication that this status should change. On the other hand, she left no doubt that change was needed in terms of the status of their pay:

This question is not for men to settle. The Lord has settled it. You are to do your duty to the women who labor in the gospel, whose work testifies that they are essential to carry the truth into families. Their work is just the work that must be done. In many respects a woman can impart knowledge to her sisters that a man cannot. The cause would suffer great loss without this kind of labor. Again and again the Lord has shown me that women teachers are just as greatly needed to do the work to which He has appointed them as are men. They should not be compelled by the sentiments and rules of others to depend upon donations for their payment, any more than should the ministers.[24]

In another statement from 1898, Ellen White talked about the same problem, and named some of the women she was concerned for as well as describing their work:

There are ministers' wives—Sisters Starr, Haskell, Wilson and Robinson—who have been devoted, earnest, whole-souled workers, giving Bible readings and praying with families, helping along by personal efforts just as successfully as their husbands. These women give their whole time, and are told that they receive nothing for their labors because their husbands receive wages. . . . These sisters are giving their time to educating those newly come to the faith.[25]

We can see from her own pen the kind of "gospel ministry" that Ellen White envisioned women doing. *In all the places where she defines or describes gospel ministry for women, she always does so in*

COPY 1

terms of this personal work, directed especially toward women and families. Of course, ordained ministers should also "visit the flock of God," but she sees in women a special suitability for this work.

Had we always made it a practice of treating women who labor in this kind of ministry more equitably, we might have seen far greater results and saved the Church much discussion and debate. Sadly, especially as a result of the financial difficulties the Church experienced during the Great Depression, the number of women serving the Church in various forms of ministry and leadership declined sharply in the 1930s.[26]

Prior to the 1930s, women held some of the highest positions of leadership in the Church. Three were Treasurers of the General Conference, many served as editor or co-editor of *The Youth's Instructor.* A number of women also served as secretary (director) of various General Conference departments or Church associations.[27] This involvement of women can and should instruct us as to how greater opportunities can be opened for women today.

Ellen White's View of the Role of Women in the Church

We have already seen that Ellen White made no explicit statement supporting (or prohibiting) ordination for women (see Chapter 7, "But What About Ellen White?"). When she had opportunity to speak for it—such as after the failure of the 1881 General Conference resolution that would have provided for it—she said nothing. When she could have called for it in connection with the pay issue for women, she did not do so. What we do find is that Ellen White believed women could and should do a great work for Christ—in all their personal associations, bringing God's special message for this time into homes and families. She recognized and cited important contributions they could make in various leadership responsibilities in the church, as well.

For example, during the same time period in which she made some of the strong appeals we have noted above, she called for training to be offered for women in Adventist schools. Speaking of Avondale, at that time a new school in Australia, she said, "The Lord designs that the school should also be a place where train-

Concordia Parish Library
Ferriday, Louisiana

ing may be gained in women's work." After listing certain domestic and educational training to be included, she adds, "They are to be qualified to take any post that may be offered—superintendents, Sabbath school teachers, Bible workers. They must be prepared to teach day schools for children."[28]

She saw an important mission for women:

> Wonderful is the mission of the wives and mothers and the younger women workers. If they will, they can exert an influence for good to all around them. By modesty in dress and circumspect deportment, they may bear witness to the truth in its simplicity. They may let their light so shine before all, that others will see their good works and glorify their Father which is in heaven. A truly converted woman will exert a powerful transforming influence for good. Connected with her husband, she may aid him in his work, and become the means of encouragement and blessing to him. When the will and way are brought into subjection to the Spirit of God, there is no limit to the good that can be accomplished.[29]

While there is surely an emphasis on a husband-wife ministry here, single women ("the younger women workers") are also included. The type of work is not here designated, but would surely include the various lines of work that Ellen White specified which we have noted already. Women may let their light shine brightly and exert a limitless influence for good. Such will be the effect when the will and way are brought into subjection to God.

A God-Appointed Sphere

Ellen White presents many ways that women can work for the Lord. She would also be the first to say that we should go to the Bible for guidance on the matter of the role relationships of men and women. "The Scriptures," she affirmed, "are plain upon the relations and rights of men and women."[30] This scriptural approach is what we have tried to take in this book.

In connection with the biblical account of the fall, for instance, Ellen White indicates that the way Adam and Eve related to each other changed dramatically after sin entered. As a result, conflicting principles now strive for the mastery within every human being and submission to God's plan is not always put first:

> Eve had been perfectly happy by her husband's side in her Eden home; but, like restless modern Eves, she was flattered with the hope of entering a higher sphere than that which God had assigned her. In attempting to rise above her original position, she fell far below it. A similar result will be reached by all who are unwilling to take up cheerfully their life duties in accordance with God's plan. In their efforts to reach positions for which He has not fitted them, many are leaving vacant the place where they might be a blessing. In their desire for a higher sphere, many have sacrificed true womanly dignity and nobility of character, and have left undone the very work that Heaven appointed them.[31]

Clearly, it is important, in Ellen White's view, to operate within the sphere that God has assigned, for our own happiness and nobility as well as to be ultimately effective. Defining that sphere is, of course, what this whole discussion is about in our Church.

Culture vs. Scripture

We are also reminded of the dangers of accepting cultural practices when they conflict with scriptural duty. Ellen White's statement that "the Scriptures are plain upon the relations and rights of men and women" comes from a passage that deals with the women's rights movement in the 1860s. Part of that movement was an attempt to bring about much-needed reform in the matter of women's dress. But the proposed alternative to the unhealthy fashions that then flourished was a style that sought to minimize the differences between the dress of men and of women.

After addressing the biblical call for a clear distinction in dress, Ellen White commented on the spirit that attended the women's rights movement:

> Those who feel called out to join the movement in favor of woman's rights and the so-called dress reform might as well sever all connection with the third angel's message. The spirit which attends

the one cannot be in harmony with the other. The Scriptures are plain upon the relations and rights of men and women.[32]

Was there a spirit of resentment, of promotion of self? In the assertion of one's rights, is there a spirit which is not from above, and that keeps us from representing the character of Jesus, who did not think equality was "a thing to be grasped" (Phil 2:6)? This statement seems to warn us of such dangers.

Respect for Husband's Leadership

Ellen White upheld, in both her practice and her teaching, the traditional understanding of the Bible's statements on the headship of man in marriage. Arthur White, Ellen White's grandson, writes:

> Her understanding of the proper relationship between husband and wife stands out in a letter written to a friend in her early married life:
>
> "We women must remember that God has placed us subject to the husband. He is the head and our judgment and views and reasonings must agree with his if possible. If not, the preference in God's Word is given to the husband where it is not a matter of conscience. We must yield to the head" [Letter 5, 1861].
>
> She would not stand in the pulpit to speak at the Sabbath morning worship service if James White was present. He would take the Sabbath morning service, and she would speak in the afternoon. Only when he was stricken with paralysis in 1865 and for some time could not take his place in public work did she depart from this procedure.[33]

In this connection, it will be helpful also to mention that Ellen White's emphasis on working within the sphere God has appointed seems to have been an attempt to encourage each individual to labor where he or she could be most effective.

"Women to Be Gospel Workers"

It is clear that Ellen White *did* see a particular sphere of work for women. In 1900, she spoke specifically of the work that women are to do, after first indicating what they are to be.

The Lord has a work for women as well as men to do. They may accomplish a good work for God if they will first learn in the school of Christ the precious, all-important lesson of meekness. They must not only bear the name of Christ, but possess His Spirit. They must walk even as He walked, purifying their souls from everything that defiles. Then they will be able to benefit others by presenting the all-sufficiency of Jesus.

Women may take their places in the work at this crisis, and the Lord will work through them. If they are imbued with a sense of their duty, and labor under the influence of the Spirit of God, they will have just the self-possession required for this time. The Saviour will reflect upon these self-sacrificing women the light of His countenance, and this will give them a power which will exceed that of men. They can do in families a work that men cannot do, a work that reaches the inner life. They can come close to the hearts of those men cannot reach. Their labor is needed.

A direct necessity is being met by the work of women who have given themselves to the Lord and are reaching out to help a needy, sin-stricken people. Personal evangelistic work is to be done. The women who take up this work carry the gospel to the homes of the people in the highways and the byways. They read and explain the word to families, praying with them, caring for the sick, relieving their temporal necessities. They present before families and individuals the purifying, transforming influence of the truth. They show that the way to find peace and joy is to follow Jesus.[34]

There is a bit more in this particular section, but these statements illustrate Ellen White's perspective on women as gospel workers. If done in the right spirit under the influence of Christ, "the light of His countenance . . . will give them a power which will exceed that of men. . . . Their labor is needed."[35]

This is the very concern that we hear expressed today by those who would like to see women serving in the ordained ministry of the church—that their ministry is needed, especially to women and families. Clearly, Ellen White shared that concern, but it is also quite clear that she envisioned this ministry being performed by women without reference to their serving as ordained elders or ordained ministers. She said that such ministry, when rightly done, is capable of exhibiting a power greater than that of men. It is noble work, and a needed work.

A Revolutionizing Plan

Did Ellen White call for ordaining women as elders or ordained ministers? No. Did she explicitly forbid it? No. She simply didn't address it directly as an issue. But it also seems clear that she did not envision it.

What she did envision is significant: apart from the matter of ordination, she urged a vigorous participation of women, especially in personal ministry—one that is not yet being widely done and that the Adventist Church needs desperately.

What difference would our adoption of Ellen White's view of the role of women in the church make? It calls for no change in church structure or polity, yet its implementation would revolutionize the church's practice.

▸ When women are encouraged to work in the spirit of Jesus in harmony with their God-given roles, light from Jesus "will give them a power which will exceed that of men."[36]

▸ There would be a great increase in personal work being done, by both paid full- and part-time workers as well as by volunteers.

▸ There would be an explosion in the numbers of people won to Christ and His truth through the gentle, appealing ministry of women.

▸ There would be healing in the home relationships, as godly women workers encouraged men to reflect the self-sacrificing headship of Christ in their own relationships with their wives, and women to honor that headship as they would the headship of Christ, unless it would conflict with conscience.

▶ Families would be strengthened, and the church would make a start on the road to showing a world filled with hurting and broken families what a difference the practice of the Lordship of Jesus in loving service really makes.

But what about certain parts of the church that are divided on the subject of women's ordination? What role should culture play in our decisions on this issue? The next chapter examines Acts 15 to see if we can find some principles that will help us answer these questions.

Endnotes:

1. Ellen G. White, *Evangelism* (Washington, D.C.: Review and Herald, 1946), 472 (Ms. 43a, 1898, in *Manuscript Releases*, 21 vols. [Washington, D.C. and Hagerstown, MD: Review and Herald, 1981-1993], vol. 1, 325, 326).

2. White, *Evangelism*, 492, 493.

3. See the vivid account of Mrs. Henry's mental struggle, final acceptance of the Sabbath, and baptism in Margaret White-Thiele, *Whirlwind of the Lord* (Hagerstown, Md.: Review and Herald, 1998), 222-237.

4. Laurel Damsteegt, "S. M. I. Henry: Pioneer in Women's Ministry," *Adventists Affirm*, vol. 9 (Spring 1995), 17-19, 46.

5. Mary Henry Rossiter, *My Mother's Life: The Evolution of a Recluse* (Chicago, IL: Revell, 1900), 300-302, 308, 309.

6. Douglas Morgan, "Henry, Sarepta Myrenda Irish," in *The Ellen G. White Encyclopedia*, ed. Denis Fortin and Jerry Moon (Hagerstown, MD: Review and Herald, 2013), 408.

7. Rossiter, *My Mother's Life*, 329, 330; White-Thiele, *Whirlwind of the Lord*, 284.

8. Rossiter, *My Mother's Life*, 329.

9. Ibid., 330, 331.

10. Ellen G. White, *Review and Herald*, May 9, 1899, 293, published under the title, "The Excellency of the Soul," in Mrs. Henry's column, "Woman's Gospel Work."

11. See Appendix 5, "Women Licensed as Adventist Ministers, 1869-1975."

12. White, *Review and Herald*, May 9, 1899, 293 (emphasis original).

13. Ibid.

14. Bobby Jane Van Dolson and Leo R. Van Dolson, eds., *Seventh-day Adventist Encyclopedia: A-L*, 2d rev. edition, Commentary Reference Series 10 (Hagerstown, MD: Review and Herald, 1996), 691, citing Arthur Whitefield Spalding, *Origin and History of Seventh-day Adventists* (Washington, D.C.: Review and Herald, 1962), vol. 3, 200.

15. When Ellen White herself published the material she had written to Mrs. Henry, under the title, "Women to Be Gospel Workers," she did not publish the entire letter, but reworked portions of it for general use. Her admonition to Mrs. Henry, "Address the crowd whenever you can," was not included. See Ellen G. White, *Testimonies for the Church*, 9 vols. (Mountain View, CA: Pacific Press, 1948), vol. 6, 114-116.

16. Rossiter, *My Mother's Life*, 324, 325. See also Damsteegt, "S. M. I. Henry," 19.

17. Rossiter, *My Mother's Life*, 325, 326.

18. White, Ms. 38, 1895, in *Manuscript Releases*, vol. 2, 278.

19. White, Ms. 43a, 1898, in *Manuscript Releases*, vol. 5, 323, 324.

20. Ibid., 324.

21. Ibid., 323.

22. Ibid, 324, 325.

23. Ibid, 325, 326.

24. Ibid, 325.

25. White, Letter 137, 1898, in *Manuscript Releases*, vol. 21, 360.

26. Patrick Allen, "The Depression and the Role of Women in the Seventh-day Adventist Church," *Adventist Heritage*, vol. 11, no. 2 (Fall 1986), 51, 53.

27. Ibid., 50; Roger Coon, "Ellen White's View of the Role of Women in the SDA Church," 2, 3, http://text.egwwritings.org/publication.php?pubtype=Book&bookCode=EGWVRWSDA&pagenumber=1&paragraphReferences=1 (accessed March 16, 2015).

28. White, *Evangelism*, 475.

29. Ibid., 467, 468.

30. White, *Testimonies*, vol. 1, 421.

31. Ellen G. White, *Patriarchs and Prophets* (Mountain View, CA: Pacific Press, 1958), 59.

32. White, *Testimonies*, vol. 1, 421.

33. Arthur L. White, "Ellen G. White the Person," *Spectrum*, vol. 4, no. 2 (Spring 1972), 20. See also White, *Testimonies*, vol. 1, 306, 307, describing the duty of the husband to show a Christlike headship in his home.

34. White, *Testimonies*, vol. 6, 117, 118.

35. Ibid., 117.

36. Ibid.

NINE

WHAT WE CAN LEARN FROM ACTS 15

In Acts 15, we read how the early Church successfully dealt with a potentially very divisive issue—circumcision. The earliest Christians were, of course, Jewish. But following Pentecost, the good news spread quickly to the Gentiles, and it soon became clear that more Gentiles than Jews were becoming Christians.

Problems began when some of the Jewish Christians, "of the sect of the Pharisees" (Acts 15:5), traveled from Jerusalem to Antioch to demand that Gentile converts be required to keep the Jewish ceremonial laws, including circumcision. These Pharisaic Christians continued to believe in the temple, its services, and its laws. In their view, Gentile believers had to be circumcised in order to be saved (Acts 15:1). So it was a theological issue that was at stake.

We read in verse 2 that Paul and Barnabas had "no small dissension and dispute with them," and in the end, the visitors from Jerusalem had created quite a stir in the church at Antioch, influencing Jewish Christians and alienating Gentile Christians. At last the Church decided to send Paul and Barnabas, along with other delegates, to Jerusalem, where they would meet with the apostles and elders to discuss this question.

Along the way to Jerusalem, "they passed through Phoenicia and Samaria, describing the conversion of the Gentiles; and they caused great joy to all the brethren. And when they had come to

Jerusalem, they were received by the Church and the apostles and the elders; and they reported all things that God had done with them. But some of the . . . Pharisees who believed rose up, saying, 'It is necessary to circumcise them, and to command them to keep the law of Moses'" (vss. 3-5).

Decision Based on Scripture and Divine Revelation

The Jerusalem Council listened to all sides of the issue. However, because it was a theological matter, their decision was based exclusively on the Old Testament Scriptures and God's revelation given three times to Peter in vision (see Acts 10).

After Peter reminded the council about his rooftop vision and experience with Cornelius, he declared: "we believe that through the grace of the Lord Jesus Christ we shall be saved in the same manner as they" (vs. 11). In other words—and this is a key point—the Jewish Christians were no longer required to keep the old ceremonial laws, and the Gentile Christians were not required to keep them either!

Paul and Barnabas then shared how God had worked through them, performing "many miracles and wonders among the Gentiles" (vs. 12). Following their testimony, the entire room became quiet, and James, the chairman of the Jerusalem Council spoke:

Men and brethren, listen to me: Simon [Peter] has declared how God at the first visited the Gentiles to take out of them a people for His name. And with this the words of the prophets agree, just as it is written:

"After this I will return

And will rebuild the tabernacle of David,

which has fallen down;

I will rebuild its ruins,

And I will set it up;

So that the rest of mankind may seek the Lord,

Even all the Gentiles who are called by My name,

Says the Lord who does all these things.

Known to God from eternity are all His works."

Therefore I judge that we should not trouble those from among the Gentiles who are turning to God, but that we write to them to abstain from things polluted by idols, from sexual immorality, from things strangled, and from blood. (vss. 13-20).

After the Jerusalem Council

Everyone at the council agreed that this was a good solution, and a letter was written explaining this decision. In addition, the Gentile believers were "urged to keep the commandments and to lead holy lives. They were also to be assured that the men who had declared circumcision to be binding were not authorized to do so by the apostles."[1]

Paul and Barnabas, along with Judas and Silas, were sent to Antioch, where they shared the letter with the believers there, assuring both Gentile and Jewish Christians that circumcision was not required of any Christian.

Key Points

As we consider this situation of Church conflict and resolution as recorded in Acts 15, here are some key points to keep in mind:

1. The Jerusalem Council did not establish two different standards based on culture—one for Jewish believers and another for Gentiles. The decision of the council pertained to all Christians everywhere—both Jewish and Gentile believers in Christ. And because of that, the result was a unified Church worldwide.

2. The Jerusalem Council did not institutionalize a division in the Church between Jews and Gentiles; in fact, it did just the opposite. They reaffirmed that Christ's death on the Cross broke down the wall between Jews and Gentiles: "For He Himself is our peace, who made both groups into one and broke down the barrier of the dividing wall, by abolishing in His flesh the enmity, which is the Law of commandments contained in ordinances, so that in Himself He might make the two into one new man, thus establishing peace" (Eph. 2:14, 15).

In other words, by its decision, the Jerusalem Council declared that there was no such thing as Jew or Gentile anymore, and that all had to live by the same laws—the laws of the kingdom of heaven, as one people, united in Christ.

3. The Jerusalem Council shows us that when there is disagreement and dissension in the Church, we are not to look to our own culture for wisdom and guidance. Instead, God provides a solution based on Scripture and divine revelation.

Just as He used Scripture and divine revelation in directing the early Church through difficult issues, the same God—who does not change (Mal. 3:6)—uses the same methods to guide His Church today.

Circumcision and Culture

Some have suggested that the situation facing the early Church over circumcision is similar to the debate regarding women's ordination. They suggest that the Jerusalem Council allowed for "two systems of evangelism" based upon culture—one for the circumcised and another for the uncircumcised.

But as we have already seen, the early Church stayed united by making its decision using Scripture and divine revelation—not culture. Neither Gentiles *nor* Jews were required to be circumcised. As Paul later wrote, "Circumcision is nothing and uncircumcision is nothing, but keeping the commandments of God *is what matters*" (1 Cor. 7:19).

Circumcision was not based on culture; it was a sign given by God to Abraham, "a seal of the righteousness of the faith which he had while still uncircumcised, that he might be the father of all those who believe . . ." (Rom. 4:11).

Like the ceremonial law, circumcision was a shadow pointing forward to the gift of the Spirit and the new birth, symbolized by baptism. Peter indicates as much in his speech to the Jerusalem Council: God was "giving them [Gentiles] the Holy Spirit, just as He also did to us [Jews]; and He made no distinction between us and them, cleansing their hearts by faith" (Acts 15:8, 9). Like the ceremonial law, circumcision was a "shadow of things to come" and came to an end with the death of Christ and God's rending of the temple veil from top to bottom.

Ordination and Culture

So is gender-exclusive ordination to the gospel ministry based on culture? Not according to the Bible or Ellen White, as we have seen in earlier chapters (see 1 Tim. 2:12, 13 and chapters 6-8 of this book).

Ordination to the gospel ministry in the New Testament Church was begun by Jesus Himself in ordaining the twelve apostles. Later, through the writings of Paul, He continued to guide the Church in the selection of spiritual leaders (see 1 Tim. 3:1-13 and Titus 1:5-9). Unlike circumcision, which was given by God as a temporary sign to Abraham and his descendants, the gender-exclusive roles of minister and elder were given by God to His Church, based on the Creation order leadership model that He established in the Garden of Eden.

The table below summarizes the differences between Creation order leadership and circumcision:

Creation Order Leadership	Circumcision
From Eden, like the Sabbath and the family	From Israel, like the ceremonial law
Began with Adam, father of the human race	Began with Abraham, father of the Jews
Like the Sabbath, points back to Eden	Like the ceremonial law, points forward
Godly leadership model	Foreshadowed baptism
Reality	Shadow
Unchangeable, for the Church in all ages	Temporary, ended with the death of Christ

It's helpful to notice that

- ▶ Unlike the Sabbath, the family, and Creation order leadership, circumcision was not instituted in the Garden of Eden.

- ▶ Circumcision began with Abraham, who was the father of the Hebrews.

- ▶ Circumcision is connected with the ceremonial law, unlike the Sabbath and Creation order leadership which cannot be changed (Acts 15:5).

Significance for Today

Because the issue we are facing today is *theological* and connected with the *Creation order*, it is far greater than the question of whether or not a woman should be ordained as a gospel minister overseeing the Church. *The issue is whether Scripture or culture will guide the Church.* As we have seen, the Bible is clear—both Old and New Testaments—and if we compromise our faithfulness to Scripture on this point, we will have given up our only secure basis for unity.

As much as we appreciate diversity, *it is Scripture—our Bible-based faith and practice—that holds us together as a world Church*, not diversity. It is this Bible-based unity that will protect us from the scourges of pluralism and enable us to weather the storms of the last days. Our confidence in the unity of Scripture can only be maintained if we continue to interpret it in the way the Bible interprets itself. If we begin to interpret it differently in different places, there is nothing to keep the church from splintering over tithe, congregationalism, homosexuality, and other issues.

Just as the Sabbath and marriage cannot be compromised without compromising the unity of the Church, neither can the Creation order leadership given in Genesis and affirmed by Paul, because it applies to self-sacrificing leadership in the Church. That principle cannot be compromised without ultimately destroying the unity of the Church. If we allow diversity here, it will divide us. It already *has* divided us to some extent.

When Israel demanded a king, rejecting God's kingship and His plan for leadership over them, Israel was divided, and ultimately, Israel was destroyed. The Jerusalem Council made its decision based on Scripture and divine revelation, and the New Testament Church not only remained united; it continued to grow stronger and stronger, "turning the world upside down" (Acts 17:6). As we remain faithful to God and His word, the same will be true for us today.

Endnote:

1. Ellen G. White, *The Acts of the Apostles* (Mountain View, CA: Pacific Press, 1911), 195.

TEN

DOES THE BIBLE SUPPORT WOMEN'S ORDINATION

There are many points upon which the vast majority of Seventh-day Adventists agree, even when it comes to ordination. These include the biblical teachings that Christ is the Head of the Church, that all of us as Church members are commissioned to spread the gospel, that spiritual gifts are gender-inclusive, and that men and women are fully equal because we are created in the image of God.

The Main Question

With so much agreement, it is surprising that we have not found agreement on the main question; namely, "Do the biblical qualifications for the gospel minister who oversees the Church allow a woman to be ordained to this office?" The preceding chapters have tried to make clear that the Bible does not give two different answers to this question, any more than it gives two different answers as to which day God commands us to keep holy as the Sabbath, though conservative Christians who believe the whole Bible as God's inspired Word have come to opposite conclusions on this point.[1]

Some have claimed that the question of who should be ordained to the gospel ministry is an "ecclesiological" or "ecclesiastical" question, rather than a theological question. But this is a false dichotomy, since ecclesiology ("theological doctrine relating to the church")[2] is a subset of theology and ecclesiastical ("of or relating to a church especially as an established institution"; "suitable for use in a church")[3] is driven by our theology. In other words, how we understand the Church (ecclesiology) and issues related to the way the Church functions (ecclesiastical) flow from our theology and cannot be separated from it. Therefore, at its root, the subject of ordination is definitely a theological question.

A Worldwide Church

The way some people talk, an uninformed person would think that the organizational system of the Seventh-day Adventist Church is broken. But that is not the case. The fact is that our present system of organization has worked remarkably well for over one hundred years, established on the Bible and the Spirit of Prophecy. And our worldwide system of ordination with more than 18,000 currently active ordained ministers has functioned effectively for more than 150 years.

As a result, we are the only truly worldwide Protestant Church, with a presence in 216 out of the 238 countries recognized by the United Nations and growing rapidly wherever we have fully embraced and integrated our message, mission, identity, and purpose as Seventh-day Adventists. Even a recent *Christianity Today* article described our growth in glowing terms:

> In 2014, for the 10th year in a row, more than 1 million people became Adventists, hitting a record 18.1 million members. Adventism is now the fifth largest Christian communion worldwide, after Catholicism, Eastern Orthodoxy, Anglicanism, and the Assemblies of God.[4]

Without question, Jesus raised us up as a remnant Church and has abundantly blessed our work, but this is due in large part to our faithfulness to the Scriptures and His inspired counsel. We cannot take it for granted as if it's our birthright.

Church Organization Established by Jesus

In fact, it was Jesus who established the Church from the beginning, laying a solid foundation built on "the apostles and prophets,"

He "Himself being the chief cornerstone" (Eph. 2:20). As we have seen, the twelve apostles were even organized into three subgroups of two pairs each, and through them Jesus instituted the system of Church offices, first deacons and then elders, as the Church grew. This system of ordained Church leaders enabled the early Church to spread rapidly throughout the Roman Empire and beyond.

With regard to both ordained offices (minister/elder and deacon), the Bible is clear regarding the qualifications expected of those who fill them. As 92 percent of the Theology of Ordination Study Committee agreed,[5] ordination is the biblical practice of setting apart those who meet the scriptural qualifications.[6] Paul sets forth these qualifications in 1 Timothy 3 and Titus 1—letters written to his closest co-workers who traveled widely and were given the responsibility of managing several churches. According to these biblical passages, ministers/elders who oversee the Church "must be blameless, the husband of one wife, temperate, sober-minded, of good behavior, hospitable, able to teach, not given to wine, not violent, not greedy for money, but gentle, not quarrelsome, not covetous" (1 Tim. 3:2, 3). Paul specified the same qualifications in his epistle to Titus: "if a man is blameless, the husband of one wife," etc. (Titus 1:6).

While some may say that no one perfectly meets all of these qualifications, that is not the issue. The fact is that the qualifications clearly describe the kind of spiritual leader the person "must be" if they are to fill the office of ordained minister/elder. Just because it is not one of the Ten Commandments doesn't mean it's optional or isn't important. Is the Great Commission, celebration of the Lord's Supper, and foot washing merely good advice, or are they divine commands? Once we as a Church begin disregarding clear biblical injunctions, where will it end? As a recent *Time* magazine article has pointed out:

> So far no Christian tradition has been able to embrace the LGBT [Lesbian, Gay, Bisexual, Transsexual] community without first changing its views about women. The same reasoning that concludes that homosexuality is sin is also behind the traditional evangelical view that husbands are the spiritual leaders of marriages and men are the leaders in church.[7]

The "reasoning" referred to, of course, is the conviction that the Bible is no less God's Word for us today than it was for previous generations.

Scripture Is the Authority

We are not free to pick and choose the portions of Scripture we want to follow. The question as to the "appropriateness" of ordaining women to the gospel ministry is an inappropriate question! Asking whether something is appropriate or inappropriate puts the ball in our court and grants us as human beings the power to decide what is right or not for our time and area of the world.

Once we recognize that there are biblical qualifications for the office of the gospel minister who oversees the Church, then who are we to ask whether it is appropriate or not? That is like asking whether it is appropriate that Jesus chose twelve apostles or tells us to "make disciples of all nations" (Matt. 28:19). God has not given these matters into our hands to decide, which is why He specified them in His Word. His Word has always been and must remain the authoritative basis for our faith *and practice*.

Our Main Findings

The Bible is clear regarding God's will for the spiritual leadership of His Church. To briefly recap what we have seen in previous chapters:

▸ The requirement that the gospel minister who oversees the Church "must be the husband of one wife" (1 Tim. 3:2) is as clear in the original Greek as it is in English. The Greek word for "husband" never means a female and the word for "wife" never means a male. Rather, as 57 of 61 English translations over the past 700 years affirm, these are clear gender requirements that cannot be avoided unless we redefine what we mean by male and female. But that has already been defined by God at Creation when He made Adam and Eve.

▸ Paul moves from gender-inclusive language ("all people") and gender-specific terms (*men* and *women*) in 1 Timothy

2 to gender-exclusive language ("husband of one wife")
in 1 Timothy 3 in connection with Church offices. His
reference to "the women" who assisted the deacons in
1 Timothy 3:11 is further proof that the gender-exclusive
language is intentional.

▶ Although there are at least five command forms in Greek,
Paul employs the strongest one when he says that the
minister/elder *must be* (*dei . . . einai* in Greek). It's the
form used to indicate a divine imperative (e.g., Matt. 24:6;
Mark 13:10; Luke 24:44; John 3:14; Acts 4:12; 1 Cor. 15:53;
2 Cor. 5:10; Heb. 11:6, Rev. 22:6).

▶ Women are just as vital as men to the growth of the
Church. Paul's command that women "keep silent" in
Church is directed at women who were disrupting the
worship service by asking questions. In addition to this
group, the same command is given to two groups *of
men* who were being disruptive (see 1 Cor. 14:27-33). In
1 Timothy 2:11, 12, Paul prohibits women usurping an
authoritative teaching role, as our Adventist pioneers
recognized and taught, including Ellen White.[8]

▶ The New Testament provides rules or codes of conduct for
both the home and the Church. In the home, wives are to
submit to their husbands, and husbands are to love their
wives; children are to obey their parents, and fathers are
not to provoke their children. For the Church too, which
is "the household of God," there are rules for worship and
for filling Church offices. There should be no "headless
horsemen" in the Church!

▶ Ellen White was never ordained to a Church office. The
Church issued her the highest credentials available, as a
recognition of her special calling as "the Lord's messenger"
and as a practical way of granting her full access to pulpits
worldwide.

▶ The issue in Acts 15 (whether Gentiles must be
circumcised to be saved) was theological. Circumcision

was a ceremonial requirement. It was not like the Sabbath and Creation order leadership, which were established before the Fall and valid for God's people everywhere in all ages.

The Way Forward

When the early Church was threatened with division as a result of some who were determined to push the issue of circumcision on the whole Church, the Jerusalem Council, consisting of the apostles and elders representing the various churches, resolved matters by issuing a Bible-based decision that was to be followed by all believers everywhere. In a similar way, as Seventh-day Adventists, we have always been a Bible-based Church and have been clearly advised by inspiration that "Before accepting any doctrine or precept, we should demand a plain 'Thus saith the Lord' in its support."[9]

We believe the Bible is plain. It does not require a doctorate in theology or sophisticated methods of interpretation to understand. We also believe that the Bible is consistent throughout. Paul neither contradicts himself nor has he misunderstood Genesis. The pattern of male leadership spans the entire Bible, from Adam's leadership in the Garden of Eden and the patriarchs and priests of the Old Testament to Jesus' establishment of the apostles and elders in the New Testament, culminating in the New Jerusalem, where the gates are inscribed with the names of the twelve tribes of Israel and the foundations bear the names of the twelve apostles (Rev. 21:12-14).

If we ever come to the place as a Church where we can interpret "husband of one wife" to mean "wife of one husband" or simply "faithful man or woman," then we can make any passage of Scripture mean whatever we want it to mean or whatever our culture tells us it should mean. Could it be that, as a Church, we are now being tested as to whether we will continue to maintain the Bible as the authority for our faith and practice so that, having passed this test, we will be prepared for the greater tests just ahead with regard to same-sex marriage and even the Sabbath? As the Theology of Ordination: Position No. 1 report to the Annual Council stated:

Our confidence in the unity of Scripture can only be maintained if we continue to interpret it in the way the Bible interprets itself. If we begin to interpret it differently in different places, there is nothing to keep the church from splintering over tithe, congregationalism, homosexuality, and other issues.[10]

More important even than whether or not we allow women to be ordained to the gospel ministry is how we read the Bible. As has become self-evident, some Adventists are beginning to interpret it very differently. So it's not surprising that they arrive at very different conclusions. Adventists have always been "people of the Book." We have never relied on a "magisterium" or other group to interpret the Bible for the rest of the Church. Each member is encouraged to study and know the Bible for him/herself. We know that as we approach the last days this will be especially important, so that each of us will be "ready to give . . . a reason for the hope that is in you" (1 Pet. 3:15).

In the end, what matters most is not how theologians or Church leaders at various levels interpret the Bible, but, as Jesus said, "How readest thou?" (Luke 10:26, KJV). Significantly, the question put to the 2015 General Conference Session in San Antonio is directed to *each delegate individually*:

> After *your* prayerful study on ordination from the Bible, the writings of Ellen G. White, and the reports of the study commissions; and after *your* careful consideration of what is best for the church and the fulfillment of its mission, is it acceptable for division executive committees, as they may deem it appropriate in their territories, to make provision for the ordination of women to the gospel ministry? Yes or No.[11]

Just like the early Church in Acts 15, we have always, as Adventists, made important theological decisions at General Conference sessions, trusting that God through His Word and the illumination of the Holy Spirit will guide us as to what His will is. And the result has always been a strengthening of our unity and a deepening of our understanding, notwithstanding the forces that would try to splinter or divide us.

Just as important perhaps as the decision made at a General Conference session is what we decide to do with it. Will we accept the voice of the General Conference in session as reflecting the will of God? While it is true that "Never should the mind of one man or the minds of a few men be regarded as sufficient in wisdom and power to control the work and to say what plans shall be followed," inspiration urges us to believe that a higher authority is guiding us as a Church, as the next part of this testimony explains:

But when, in a General Conference, the judgment of the brethren assembled from all parts of the field is exercised, private independence and private judgment must not be stubbornly maintained, but surrendered. Never should a laborer regard as a virtue the persistent maintenance of his position of independence, contrary to the decision of the general body.

At times, when a small group of men entrusted with the general management of the work have, in the name of the General Conference, sought to carry out unwise plans and to restrict God's work, I have said that I could no longer regard the voice of the General Conference, represented by these few men, as the voice of God. But this is not saying that the decisions of a General Conference composed of an assembly of duly appointed, representative men from all parts of the field should not be respected. God has ordained that the representatives of His church from all parts of the earth, when assembled in a General Conference, shall have authority. The error that some are in danger of committing is in giving to the mind and judgment of one man, or of a small group of men, the full measure of authority and influence that God has vested in His church in the judgment and voice of the General Conference assembled to plan for the prosperity and advancement of His work.[12]

Two years later, in 1911, Ellen White affirmed that "God has invested His church with special authority and power which no one can be justified in disregarding and despising, for he who does this despises the voice of God."[13] The secret of our unity has ever been our faithfulness to Scripture. As valuable as diversity may be, *it is our Bible-based faith and practice that holds us together.*

May we always be found faithful to God's Word, individually and as a Church. Then the Lord will bless us "exceedingly abundantly above all that we ask or think" (Eph. 3:20) and, as foretold, pour out the Holy Spirit in latter rain power to finish His work.

Endnotes:

1. See Charles P. Arrand, Craig L. Blomberg, Skip MacCarty, and Joseph A. Pipa, *Perspectives on the Sabbath: Four Views*, ed. Christopher John Donato (Nashville. TN: B&H, 2011), which includes a chapter by Seventh-day Adventist writer Skip MacCarty.

2. Merriam-Webster Online Dictionary, www.merriam-webster. com/dictionary/ecclesiology (accessed March 23, 2015).

3. Ibid., www.merriam-webster.com/dictionary/ecclesiastical (accessed March 23, 2015).

4. Sarah Eekhoff Zylstra, "The Season of Adventists: Can Ben Carson's Church Stay Separatist amid Booming Growth?" *Christianity Today*, vol. 59, no. 1 (January-February 2015), 18.

5. "Study Committee Votes Consensus Statement on 'Theology of Ordination,'" *Adventist Review* [Aug. 15, 2013], page 8), http:// news.adventist.org/all-news/news/go/2013-07-23/study-committee-votes-consensus-statement-on-theology-of-ordination/ (accessed March 19, 2015).

6. See "Consensus Statement on a Seventh-day Adventist Theology of Ordination," https://www.adventistarchives.org/consensus-statement-on-a-seventh-day-adventist-theology-of-ordination.pdf (accessed March 17, 2015).

7. Elizabeth Dias, "A Change of Heart: Inside the Evangelical War Over Gay Marriage," *Time*, January 26, 2015, 47. According to Russell Moore, president of the Southern Baptist Convention's Ethics and Religious Liberty Commission, "It is not an accident that the women's-liberation movement preceded the gay-liberation movement" (Ibid.).

8. She deferred to Elder S. N. Haskell to explain what these passag-

es meant (see Letter 17a, 1880, in *Manuscript Releases*, 21 vols. [Washington, D.C. and Hagerstown, MD: Review and Herald, 1981-1993], vol. 10, 70).

9. Ellen G. White, *The Great Controversy* (Mountain View, CA: Pacific Press, 1950), 595.

10. See Clinton Wahlen, "Theology of Ordination: Position No. 1," *Adventist Review*, http://www.adventistreview.org/church-news/theology-of-ordination-position-no.-1 (accessed March 18, 2015), given in Appendix 6.

11. Andrew McChesney, "Women's Ordination Goes to San Antonio," *Adventist Review*, November 20, 2014, 18.

12. Ellen G. White, *Testimonies for the Church*, 9 vols. (Mountain View, CA: Pacific Press, 1948), vol. 9, 260, 261.

13. Ellen G. White, *The Acts of the Apostles* (Mountain View, CA: Pacific Press, 1911), 164.

ELEVEN

MORE QUESTIONS AND ANSWERS

General Questions

1. **Is ordination really biblical, or is it an ecclesiological issue—that is, something invented by the Church and which it can therefore adapt and modify?**

As the Consensus Statement on a Seventh-day Adventist Theology of Ordination affirms, a document approved by 92 percent of the General Conference Theology of Ordination Study Committee (GC-TOSC), and overwhelmingly endorsed by the General Conference Executive Committee at the 2014 Annual Council,[1]

The Scriptures identify certain specific leadership positions that were accompanied by the Church's public endorsement for persons who meet the biblical qualifications (Num. 11:16, 17; Acts 6:1-6; 13:1-3; 14:23; 1 Tim. 3:1-12; Titus 1:5-9). Several such endorsements are shown to involve "the laying on of hands." English versions of the Scriptures use the word *ordain* to translate many different Greek and Hebrew words having the basic idea of *select* or *appoint* that describe the placement of these persons in their respective offices. Over the course of Christian history the term *ordination* has acquired meanings beyond what these words originally implied. Against such a backdrop, Seventh-day Adventists understand ordination, in a biblical sense, as the action of the Church in publicly recognizing those whom the Lord has called and equipped for local and global Church ministry.[2]

2. Even our Church's best theologians can't agree on this topic, so could it be that the Bible just isn't clear on this?

Let's remember that the Bible is God's Word to us. Jesus Himself tells us, "Man shall not live by bread alone, but by every word that proceeds from the mouth of God" (Matt. 4:4). The Psalmist declares, "Your word is a lamp to my feet and a light to my path" (Ps. 119:105). No one needs a Ph.D. to understand the Bible, nor do we need someone to "interpret" the Bible for us. The only requirement is an open and willing heart, asking for the guidance of the Holy Spirit as we search the Scriptures. Jesus said, "the Holy Spirit, whom the Father will send in My name, He will teach you all things" (John 14:26) and "guide you into all truth" (16:13). In fact, God holds each of us accountable to interpret the Bible accurately (2 Tim. 3:17).

Throughout much of Christian history, the Church kept the Bible inaccessible to the people by locking it up in Latin, even physically chaining it to the building and making it a crime for regular folk to read it for themselves.[3] The Church also controlled the universities of the time. Many men, such as Martin Luther, William Tyndale, Oliver Cromwell, and others, have suffered and/or become martyrs so that people could have access to the Bible in their own languages. If the Bible is so unclear, why such commitment to make sure it was accessible to everyone?

3. Why do some people think ordination is so important, even though it's not one of the 28 Fundamental Beliefs?

The Bible is fundamental to all of our beliefs as Seventh-day Adventists, and while there is not one specific fundamental belief dedicated to the topic of ordination, the biblical principles of this practice are expressed in several of our Fundamental Beliefs, beginning with our view of Scripture as given in Fundamental Belief No. 1, which indicates that "the Holy Scriptures are the infallible revelation of His will." If they are incomplete or unclear on some points, then how can they be infallible? Fundamental Belief No. 14 states that "distinctions of race, *culture*, learning, and nationality, and differences between high and low, rich and poor, *male and female*, must not be *divisive* among us."[4] Yet, calls for a greater sensitivity to certain cultural settings and perceived injustices have made this a very divisive issue among us for more than forty years. Fundamental Belief No. 17 mentions "pastoral, evangelistic, apostolic, and teaching ministries," and refers to 1 Timothy 3:1-13, in which Paul lists the biblical qualifications for elders/ministers who oversee the Church, deacons, and the women who assist them. From the early years of the Adventist movement, this and many other Bible passages have provided the inspired foundation for our system of Church order and ordination to the gospel ministry. Our ecclesiology—our understanding of the church and how it functions—flows out of our theology, both of which are based on Scripture.

4. What is the relationship between God's call and ordination?

Jesus called many disciples to follow Him, but He only selected and ordained twelve as "apostles" (Mark 3:13-19), meaning "those sent/commissioned" just as Jesus Himself was sent/commissioned by the Father (John 17:20, 21; 20:21; Heb. 3:1, 2). While everyone is called to be a follower of Jesus and to share the gospel with others (Matt. 28:18-20; Rev. 14:6, 7; 22:17), some are appointed/ordained to the leadership offices of elder and deacon (1 Tim. 3:1-13; Titus 1:5-9) to help organize the fulfillment of the Church's mission. Qualifications are listed for each of these offices, and among the qualifications in each case is the specification that the person should be male (apostle, Acts 1:21 ["of these *men*," using the plural of the Greek word *anēr*, "man"]; elder, 1 Tim. 3:2 ["*husband* of one wife"]; deacons, 1 Tim. 3:12 ["*husbands* of one wife"]). God uses all of us in the fulfillment of His work and has also clearly indicated the qualities that should be evident in those He calls to the Church leadership offices.

5. Is there a difference between ordination in Old Testament Israel and the New Testament Church?

In the Old Testament, priests were ordained by being anointed with oil to minister in the sanctuary and to fulfill the sacrificial rituals given by God as symbolizing atonement for sin. The Levites were set apart by the laying on of hands for their work in connection with the sanctuary. Prophets, with one exception (1 Kings 19:16), were ordained directly by God, and so no such ritual was needed. The offices of priest and Levite are not perpetuated in the New Testament Church, because type met antitype in the death of Christ as "the Lamb of God who takes away the sin of the world" (John 1:29), and Jesus ministers in the heavenly sanctuary as our High Priest (Heb. 8:1, 2). Instead, Jesus ordained the apostles as leaders of His Church (cf. Eph. 2:20), and they, in turn, ordained elders and deacons as Church leaders through prayer and the laying on of hands. For more details on this subject, see Chapter 2, "Is Ordination Biblical?" and Chapter 4, "The Husband of One Wife . . . Really?"

6. How does ordination relate to spiritual gifts?

There are several lists of spiritual gifts in the New Testament, which together reflect a wide diversity of talents put to spiritual use. These include prophecy, evangelism, teaching, administration, helps, hospitality, ministry to the poor, and many others (Rom. 12:6-8; 1 Cor. 12:4-10, 28; Eph. 4:11-13; 1 Pet. 4:10, 11). Such gifts are available to both men and women, in accordance with the Spirit's choosing, bestowal, and direction (1 Cor. 12:11). These gifts include the gift of pastoring or shepherding, which is an important quality for the elder/minister who oversees the church (John 21:16; Acts 20:28; 1 Pet. 5:1-4), but may also be exercised by others. Many roles in the Church, including that of prophet (Luke 2:36; Acts 21:9; cf. 2:17, 18; 1 Cor. 11:5) are also open to women. But in the New Testament women are never seen functioning as ministers or elders. Some, however, like Priscilla with her husband Aquila, certainly could be involved in the work of nurturing new believers as well as instructing and making disciples. After all, the commission to share the gospel is something all Christians should be actively engaged in.

7. Does God ordain women to Church office?

Nowhere in the Bible is a woman ever mentioned as occupying one of the leadership offices (priest, Levite, apostle, elder, or deacon). Some think Phoebe might have been a deacon (Rom. 16:1), though the Greek words *diakonos* and *diakoneō* are frequently used in a general way to refer to anyone who serves the Lord as a member of His Church (e.g., Matt. 25:44; 27:55; John 12:26; 1 Cor. 3:5; Col. 4:7; Heb. 6:10) and only rarely in the more specific, technical sense of "deacon" (Phil. 1:1; 1 Tim. 3:8, 10, 12). Where we might expect to find women deaconesses (1 Tim. 3:11), no title is given to these women assistants. In Adventist history, there were at least two occasions in Australia when deaconesses were ordained, but the practice was short-lived and does not seem to have been widespread.[5]

8. Are women prohibited from teaching roles in the Church?

No. In 1 Timothy 2:12, the pair of infinitives "to teach" and "to have authority" are linked together in the stipulation "I do not permit" and refer to Paul's prohibition of women exercising an *authoritative* teaching role over a man in the church. In other words, each local congregation should be overseen by a biblically-qualified elder or minister (1 Tim. 3:2-7), who is responsible to "preach the word" (2 Tim. 4:2) and ensure that "sound doctrine" characterizes all the Church's teaching activities (Titus 1:9). Paul grounds this practice not in culture or custom but in the Genesis account of Creation and the Fall (see 1 Tim. 2:13-15). Women are encouraged to be supportive of God's divine order for Church leadership. Within this arrangement, women may have many different teaching roles, in Sabbath School classes, seminars, preaching, etc.

9. Wasn't the submission of women to their husbands made necessary by sin?

Submission is a far-reaching biblical principle, epitomized by Jesus' submission to the Father. While on earth, Jesus never ceased to be God.[6] He remained equal to the Father, yet He submitted His will to the Father's will (Matt. 25:39; John 8:29). Even at the end of time, when all things have been brought into subjection to Christ, the Son Himself will also be subject to Him who put all things under Him, that God may be all in all" (1 Cor. 15:28). Therefore, submission, biblically understood and practiced, in no way diminishes full equality, nor does it compromise one's value or personhood.

In Ephesians 5:21–6:9, Paul describes several asymmetrical household relationship pairs in which submission is necessary to maintain order (husband-wife, father-children, master-servant), but also qualifies how this submission is to function. The Christian husband is to love his wife as Christ loves the Church and provide for her (5:25, 28, 29), and the wife is to respect her husband (5:33) and to submit to him "as is fitting in the Lord" (Col. 3:18). The Christian father is not to provoke his children to wrath (6:4), and the children are to obey their parents "in the Lord," meaning that this obedience is motivated by their love for Jesus and should not conflict with their duty to God. Similar admonitions are given to temper potential abuse of the master-servant relationship (6:5-9). The fact that Paul quotes Genesis 2:24, which describes the pre-Fall relationship between Adam and Eve, underscores that the headship relation of the husband to the wife (Eph. 5:23) is not a result of sin. It is an illustration of the Creation order leadership principle, which also functions within the Church as "the household of God" (1 Tim. 3:15, ESV). See Chapter 6, "The Headless Horseman Rides Again," for a more detailed presentation of this principle.

10. Shouldn't we encourage diversity as a way to promote unity?

"Unity in diversity" is a popular phrase used in today's culture, particularly in political and social settings. The basic idea is to have "unity without uniformity and diversity without fragmentation."[7] God Himself created and loves diversity. Every individual who has ever lived is unique, and nature itself reveals vast variety and diversity. Unity is also vital. Jesus prayed that His followers "all may be one, as You, Father, are in Me, and I in You; that they also may be one in Us, that the world may believe that You sent Me" (John 17:21). The unity for which Christ prayed is based on truth, God's truth, found in His Word (see John 17:17, 19, 20). A hallmark of the Seventh-day Adventist Church from the beginning has been its unity based on Scripture, and it is this Bible-based unity that makes this denomination the only truly worldwide Protestant Church. Diversity in belief about what the Scriptures teach does not bring about unity, but fragmentation. Jesus said, "And if a house is divided against itself, that house cannot stand" (Mark 3:25).

The importance of a truth-based unity is also underscored by Ellen G. White: "Men would effect a union through conformity to popular opinions, through a compromise with the world. But truth is God's basis for the unity of his people."[8] And again: "We cannot purchase peace and unity at the cost of truth. The conflict may be long and painful, but at any cost we must hold fast to the Word of God."[9]

11. Doesn't God's permitting Israel to have a king suggest that there's room for flexibility in terms of Church leadership?

This idea overlooks several important facts. First, God, through Moses, had already made provision for Israel to have a king by spelling out the laws (or rules) by which godly kingship was to function in Israel (Deut. 17:14-20). Second, this brazen departure from the ideal will of God quickly led to Israel being divided and, eventually, destroyed. In the New Testament, no similar provision is made for deviation from the elder-deacon model established for the Church. Just as Paul and Barnabas ordained elders in every church they established, Paul commands Titus to do the same in every town on the island of Crete (Titus 1:5). This leadership model is necessary for Church growth and to remain united and strong—as we can see from Paul's warnings to Timothy and Titus about choosing elders carefully (1 Tim. 3:6; 5:22; Titus 1:9).

12. Doesn't the Jerusalem Council's decision prove that unity can be preserved even when different practices prevail in different places?

A common misperception is that the Jerusalem Council in Acts 15 decided to allow for different practices among Christians in different places. This is not the case. Some of the Jewish Christians, who were "of the sect of the Pharisees" (vs. 5), were insisting that Gentile believers must be circumcised to be saved. Therefore, a theological issue was at stake. The Jerusalem Council listened to all sides of the issue but, because it was a theological matter, their decision was based exclusively on the Scriptures and God's revelation given to Peter in vision (see Acts 10). After Peter reminded the council about his rooftop vision and experience with Cornelius, he declared, "We believe that through the grace of the Lord Jesus Christ *we shall be saved in the same manner as they*" (Acts 15:11). In other words, the Jewish Christians were no longer required to keep the old ceremonial laws, and the Gentile Christians were not required to keep them either! *So the decision of the Jerusalem Council was that the requirements for both Jewish and Gentile Christians were the same:* "to abstain from things polluted by idols, from sexual immorality, from things strangled, and from blood" (Acts 15:20). For more about the Jerusalem Council, see Chapter 9, "What We Can Learn From Acts 15."

13. Doesn't Christ's headship preclude any other headship role in the Church?

There is no disagreement among Seventh-day Adventists about Christ being the Head of the Church (Eph. 5:23). On this we all agree. This does not mean, however, that Jesus does not have "undershepherds" and "overseers," who are appointed to lead the Church on earth under His headship. That is why He is also described as the "Chief Shepherd" (1 Pet. 5:4). "The elders who are among you I exhort," wrote the apostle Peter. "I who am a fellow elder and a witness of the sufferings of Christ . . . : Shepherd the flock of God which is among you, serving as overseers, not by compulsion but willingly, . . . being examples to the flock" (1 Pet. 5:1-3). Biblical qualifications as to who may serve as an overseer/undershepherd are given in Titus 1 and 1 Timothy 3. For more on this topic, see Chapter 4, "The Husband of One Wife . . . Really?" and Chapter 6, "The Headless Horseman Rides Again."

Questions about Specific Bible Passages[10]

1. Doesn't Genesis 1:26-28 proclaim God's ideal of full equality for men and women?

Yes! Human beings were created in God's image (Gen. 1:26). Therefore, though different, we are all equal before God and equally loved by Him (Ps. 8:4, 5; Rom. 2:11). We are complementary, because from the beginning God differentiated human beings as male and female (Gen. 1:27). While both Adam and Eve were given dominion over the animal kingdom and all created things (Gen. 1:28; Ps. 8:6-8), we are also told that "under God, Adam was to stand at the head of the earthly family, to maintain the principles of the heavenly family."[11] Since Adam was created first, he was given responsibilities not given to Eve (Gen. 2:7, 15-19, 22, 23). Ellen White tells us that "Adam was appointed by God to be monarch of the world, under the supervision of the Creator."[12] He "was lord in his beautiful domain."[13] Adam is also called "the father and representative of the whole human family."[14] Nothing remotely similar is ever said of Eve. In fact, it was not Eve's sin that caused the fall of the human race; it was the sin of Adam (Rom. 5:12), which is why when God confronted them after their sin He looked for Adam, using the Hebrew masculine singular form ("Where art *thou*?" Gen. 3:9, KJV) and held Adam principally responsible (vss. 10, 11). Biblically understood, equality, complementarity, mutuality, and godly leadership are not contradictory.

2. Since Genesis 3:16 is after the Fall, doesn't the leadership arrangement described there come short of God's ideal for the home and the Church?

It may, but by God's grace working in the family and in the Church it doesn't have to. After Adam and Eve sinned, God indicated that there would be a power struggle. Eve's desire would now be "against" her husband (Gen. 3:16, ESV margin). The parallel in Hebrew between this verse and Genesis 4:7 is almost identical. Both describe a struggle for dominance. But just as Cain was to rule over sin, the divine plan is for man's Creation order leadership to continue: "he [Adam] shall rule over you [Eve]" (Gen. 3:16c). Whether his leadership would be predominantly positive or negative would depend on the extent to which Adam would exercise it with God's loving headship in view as well as on the woman's willingness to accept it. Sadly, as Ellen White observes, "man's abuse of the supremacy thus given him has too often rendered the lot of woman very bitter and made her life a burden." But God's redemptive intent in placing Eve in subjection to Adam was that, by their cherishing "the principles enjoined in the law of God," this leadership arrangement would be a blessing to them.[15]

3. Doesn't Genesis 5:1, 2 show that the Hebrew word for "man" ('adam) is generic, meaning "human(kind)"?

Some suggest that the Hebrew word 'adam is always used in Genesis and even the entire Hebrew Bible in a generic sense, meaning either "human being" or "humankind," not "Adam" as the name of the first man. But this ignores the fact that Scripture itself, beginning with Genesis, unambiguously refers to the name of the first man as "Adam" (Gen. 5:1, 3-5; 1 Chr. 1:1; Luke 3:38; Rom. 5:14, etc.). We must not ignore this biblical key for understanding the first four chapters of the Bible. Another key is that Genesis adds the Hebrew definite article when referring to Adam as "*the* [prototypical] man" (Gen. 1:27; 2:7, 8, 15, 16, 18-23, 25; 3:8, 9, 12, 20, 22, 24; 4:1), while it is usually left off when referring to "Adam" by name (Gen. 2:20; 3:17, 21; 4:25).[16] The only clearly generic uses of 'adam occur at the beginning and the end of the Adam narrative. In Genesis 1:26, God calls the entire human family, both male and female, "Man" ('adam).

This generic usage occurs next in Genesis 5:1, 2, acting as a bookend to its use in Genesis 1 in order to conclude the Genesis account of the earliest days of human history. But notice that, in Genesis 5, the generic use of 'adam is specifically distinguished from "Adam" as the name of the first man: "This is the book of the genealogy of Adam. In the day that God created man, He made him in the likeness of God. He created them male and female, and blessed them and called them Mankind in the day they were created" (5:1, 2).[17] In other words, sometimes 'adam refers to Adam as a human being, and sometimes it refers to Adam as the head and representative of all mankind—in harmony with Genesis 1 and 2, which shows the man being given the primary leadership role in the human family and in the family of God.[18]

4. Doesn't God promise to pour out the Spirit on both men and women, irrespective of gender, in Acts 2:17-21?

Yes! On the day of Pentecost, men and women were together in Jerusalem in obedience to Jesus' command and praying "all with one accord" (Acts 2:1) when the Holy Spirit was poured out on them (vss. 2-4). According to Peter, this was a fulfillment of the prophecy of Joel 2:28-32. "I will pour out of My Spirit on all flesh; Your sons and your daughters shall *prophesy*, Your young men shall *see visions*, Your old men shall *dream dreams*. And on My menservants and on My maidservants I will pour out My Spirit in those days; And they shall *prophesy*" (Acts 2:17-21). They were not just preachers. According to Peter, they *prophesied*; they had visions and dreams. Jesus had spoken of sending prophets to bear witness of Him (Matt. 23:34; Luke 11:49). The New Testament confirms that the gift of prophecy came upon both men and women and that it actively functioned throughout the Apostolic period. Mentioned by name as prophets are Agabus (Acts 11:27, 28; 21:10), Barnabas and others (13:1), Judas and Silas, and the four daughters of Philip (21:9), besides those in Ephesus upon whom the gift of tongues (languages) came in order to prophesy intelligibly to many different people groups (Acts 19:6; cf. 2:8-11). To use this passage to refer to last-day preaching diminishes the vital role of prophecy—God-inspired speech—to counter Satan's last-day deceptions (Rev. 12:17; cf. 16:13-15).

5. Isn't it significant that in Acts 9:36 Dorcas is called a "disciple"?

While Dorcas happens to be the only woman actually called a "disciple" in the New Testament (using the feminine form of the word in Greek, *mathētria*), clearly, other women were also disciples, beginning with the women who followed Jesus and listened to His teachings (Luke 8:1-3). Mary Magdalene is shown following the conventions of rabbinic disciples by sitting and learning at Jesus' feet, calling Him "Teacher" or "Rabbi" (Luke 10:39, 42; John 20:16) and Jesus defended her, contrary to the Jewish cultural conventions of the time. Dorcas herself "was full of good works and charitable deeds" and widows and other disciples, both men and women, lamented her death and rejoiced at her resurrection in answer to the apostle Peter's prayer. As we know, there were many women active in various kinds of ministries (see chapter 3 for examples in the Bible and chapter 8 for later examples).

6. **Don't women prophetesses like Huldah in the Old Testament, the daughters of Philip in Acts 21:9, and Ellen White in modern times prove that God calls women to the highest positions?**

The whole notion of "higher" vs. "lower" positions is fundamentally out of harmony with the teaching of the Lord Jesus, who came not to be served but to serve (Mark 10:45) and taught His disciples that the greatest in the kingdom is the one who is "last of all and servant of all" (Mark 9:35). Regarding prophets and prophetesses, throughout Scripture these individuals were called directly by God Himself, and even chosen by Him from the womb (Jer. 1:5), whereas the system of Old Testament priestly leadership was restricted to "the sons of Aaron" (Num. 3:13) and the New Testament office of elder/minister is limited to those who meet the biblical qualifications (1 Tim. 3:2-7; Titus 1:5-9). Ellen White herself never held elective church office, "was never ordained by human hands, nor did she ever perform a wedding, organize a church, or conduct a baptism."[19]

7. **Does Romans 16:1, 2 suggest that Phoebe was a deaconess or church leader?**

Some think that Phoebe was a deaconess, based on the use of the word *diakonos* in Romans 16:1. Since Paul, it is argued, called Phoebe a deacon, then the office must not exclude women. But, those making this argument assume what they seek to prove. As nearly all translations of Romans 16:1 recognize, *diakonos* is not used here in the technical sense of "deacon" (as it is, for example, in Phil. 1:1; 1 Tim. 3:8, 12), but in the much more common generic sense of "servant,"[20] whether of one another, the Church, or of God and of Christ. In the last part of Romans 16:1, Paul adds that Phoebe "has been a helper of many and of myself also." The Greek word here translated "helper" (*prostatis*) is widely understood as referring to her as a financial supporter of Paul and others (similar to many of the women who followed Jesus as mentioned in Luke 8:3). The suggestion that here it means "leader" is based on a usage of the Greek word several centuries earlier. Furthermore, it does not fit the context of this verse as it is difficult to imagine Paul considering Phoebe as his "leader"—something he refused to concede even to other apostles (2 Cor. 11:5; 12:11), including James, Peter, and John (Gal. 2:6-10).

8. Doesn't Romans 16:7 indicate that Junia was an apostle?

First of all, we do not know whether Andronicus and Junia(s) are linked because they were siblings, or a husband-and-wife team. We do not even know whether the Greek name *Iounian* is female, "Junia" (ESV, NKJV, NRSV), or male, "Junias" (RSV, NASB, WEB). Some appeal to occurrences of the name in *Latin* which refer to women, but the *Greek* form used by Paul has an ending that could be either masculine or feminine. The other instances of this ending in Romans 16 all clearly refer to men. Even if we assume that Paul refers to a woman here, he cannot mean that the two were "well-known" apostles for two reasons. First, when Paul speaks of *the* apostles (with the definite article in Greek), he refers to the apostles of Christ and others like himself, entrusted with the ministry of the Word, and whose work was attested by miraculous signs (2 Cor. 12:12); in other cases he refers to those sent by the Church for specific tasks (2 Cor. 8:19, 23; Phil. 2:25). Second, Paul avoids the clear phraseology he uses when including himself as one of the apostles (1 Cor. 15:9), using instead a Greek phrase best translated "well known to/by" the apostles (ESV, LEB). Besides, it would seem unusual that these two long-time Jewish believers and co-prisoners with Paul, apart from this brief mention, left virtually no other trace in the history of Christianity, whether in the New Testament or in early Christian tradition.[21]

9. Doesn't Paul's lengthy list of women in Romans 16 (vss. 3, 6, 12-13, 15) indicate their major role as ministers and co-workers of Paul?

As chapter 8 indicates, there are many ways in which women have and are making significant contributions. Aquila and Priscilla (or Prisca) are the husband-wife tent-making team known to us from Acts 18, who in their spare time "explained the way of God more accurately" to Apollos. Some have pointed to Paul mentioning Priscilla first as indicating that she was the dominant teacher, not her husband Aquila. However, that claim ignores the fact that Aquila is given first in Acts 18:2 when Luke introduces them and that Paul uses the same order when sending their greetings to the Corinthians (1 Cor. 16:9). The variation may be simply stylistic or influenced by the fact that their home was used for church gatherings in Ephesus and Rome (Rom. 16:5). *Tryphaena, Tryphosa,* and *Persis* "worked hard in the Lord" (vs. 12). But there is no clear evidence that any of these women, or any others for that matter, ever exercised a leadership role. Their labors appear to have been supportive of the work being carried forward by the apostles and other men whom God had called to lead His Church.

Today, God still seeks both men and women willing to fill supportive roles in the advancement of His work. Paul indicates the importance of each person's contribution to the process of readying the crop for harvest (1 Cor. 3:4-11). Every worker has an important role to play, but God gives the resultant increase so that no individual is more important than another. Equality of service is not incompatible with different roles; all are servants of Christ, and the glory belongs to God for the growth of the Church and the abundant final harvest.

10. Since Galatians 3:28 eliminates distinctions of race, class, and gender in the Church, why do we exclude women from some Church offices?

In the Church, people of all nations and races—rich and poor, highly educated and less educated, men, women, and children worship together as one family. With regard to what the apostles said to slaves and their masters, Jewish and Gentile believers found *Christian* ways to live within the laws of the Roman Empire even though slavery was never God's will—"from the beginning it was not so." In the Lord, no one is really a slave but a sister or a brother (Philem. 16).

In order to understand Galatians 3:28, it's important to remember why Paul wrote this epistle. A false gospel was being preached to the Christians in Galatia. Are we saved by keeping the law (ceremonial or moral) or by faith in Christ? Some Jewish believers were insisting that circumcision, their badge of distinctiveness as a nation, was necessary to impose on Gentile believers in order for them to be saved (Acts 15:1, 5). Even Peter began separating himself from Gentile believers when Jewish believers came to Antioch (Gal. 2:11-16). It seems that they were slow to grasp the full significance of the Cross—that Jesus, by His death, had broken down "the middle wall of separation" between Jews and Gentiles (Eph. 2:14) so that "neither circumcision nor uncircumcision avails anything, but a new creation" (Gal. 6:15; similarly, 5:6; 1 Cor. 7:19). The Jerusalem Council, by its decision, affirmed that, in God's sight, there was no such thing as Jew or Gentile anymore, and that all were to live by the same laws—the laws of the kingdom of heaven, as one people, united in Christ. Women too were to be welcomed as full-fledged members of the Church because circumcision was no longer important. What really mattered was a person's relationship to Christ: "And if you are Christ's, then you are Abraham's seed and heirs according to the promise" (Gal. 3:29).

11. According to Ephesians 5:21, aren't we all supposed to submit to each other in the Church?

Ephesians 5:21 begins a lengthy section of the epistle dealing with proper Christian behavior within the home (see also Col. 3:18–4:1; 1 Pet. 3:1-9). The command to submit to one another is then followed by a description of how individuals within the home should apply this command: wives are to submit to their husbands (vss. 22-24), husbands are to love their wives (vss. 25-33), children are to obey their parents (6:1-3), and so on. This is not a general command for everyone to submit to each other. As Christians, we are individually to submit to Christ and His will for us—in the home and in the Church. The fact that sometimes these commands have been abused is no reason to ignore them.

12. Since women like Euodia and Syntyche were coworkers with Paul (Phil. 4:1-3), doesn't that show that there were women ministers at that time.

The word translated "fellow workers" is a very general one that simply refers to those working together with or helping someone. For example, Paul calls Philemon his "fellow worker" (Philem. 1), but there is no evidence that this convert of Paul's (vs. 19) ever labored alongside Paul, though he opened his home for church meetings (vs. 2). It is curious that these women are held up as examples, since there was obviously a sharp disagreement between them that was disrupting the whole church in Philippi, requiring Paul's intervention and mediation by a Christian brother of the church. There are several better examples of women workers for the Lord in the New Testament. With these facts in mind, it is understandable that Paul specifically includes among the addressees the overseers and deacons of the church in Philippi (Phil. 1:1).

13. Isn't Paul's reference to Nympha (Col. 4:15) another example of a church led by a woman?

Like Romans 16:7, this is another case where we are unsure of whether Paul refers to a man (Nymphas) or a woman (Nympha), a fact borne out by copies of this epistle which variously refer to "his" house, "her" house, and "their" house. Even if it is a woman, it was common for well-to-do members to offer their comparatively spacious homes for church meetings, as Gaius did in Corinth (Rom. 16:23), Philemon in Colossae (Philem. 2) Lydia in Philippi (Acts 16:15, 40), and Aquila and Priscilla in several cities where they lived (1 Cor. 16:19; Rom. 16:5). We know nothing about who was actually in charge of this church.

14. Since 1 Pet. 2:9, 10 refers to all of us as priests, doesn't that mean that both men and women can be pastors?

Throughout 1 Peter, the apostle describes the Church as a new Israel in fulfillment of Old Testament expectations as to what the people of God were to be. Alluding to Exodus 19:5, 6, Peter pictures the entire body of believers as a priesthood, that they may "proclaim the praises of Him who called you out of darkness into His marvelous light" (1 Pet. 2:9). In other words, we are all given the opportunity to share the gospel with others. Elsewhere, the New Testament encourages us to offer up spiritual sacrifices, which include praise, well-doing, financial gifts (Heb. 13:15, 16), and the offering of ourselves for spreading the gospel (Rom. 12:1). As Christians, we no longer need a human priest to intercede for us; we can go directly to God in prayer through the ministry of Jesus Christ as our High Priest in the heavenly sanctuary (Matt. 6:5-8; Heb. 4:16).

15. Revelation refers to Christians as "kings and priests," so why should women not be ordained and included at all levels of Church administration?

Like Peter's reference to Christians as a "royal priesthood" (1 Peter 2:9), John describes us as a kingdom of believers (Rev. 1:6; 5:10; 20:6). This image should be understood in connection with the overall New Testament teaching that Christians have direct access to God through Christ and have no need of a human priest or mediator. Besides the summary statement in Revelation 1, Christians are called "priests" twice more (Rev. 5:10; 20:6). Both of these cases refer to the future, eternal life. Revelation 20:6 refers to the work of judgment being committed to us during the millennium. The other instance refers to our reigning as kings on the New Earth (Rev. 5:10; similarly, 22:5). In neither case does it have any relevance to Church organization, which is dealt with more specifically in Acts and the Pastoral Epistles of 1 and 2 Timothy and Titus.

Questions About Interpretation

1. Aren't many things in the Bible cultural and no longer appropriate for our time?

Most of the things in the Bible that appear cultural to us relate to Israel as a nation or to the ceremonial law of Moses. In Jesus' death on the Cross, Old Testament types and ceremonies met their fulfillment and came to an end with the rending of the temple veil (Matt. 27:51; Heb. 8:1-13; 10:19-21). The Jerusalem Council, based on divine revelation in Scripture, determined that circumcision was a ceremonial requirement and therefore no longer binding (Acts 15). Although in the early Church reverence for God and for the Creation order leadership that He established in the Church was shown by the women wearing head coverings (1 Cor. 11:4-16) and may be shown in different ways today, the principle of godly male leadership remains unchanged (vs. 3).[22]

2. **If we interpret the Bible literally, how can we reject passages in the Bible that condone slavery, but accept passages that exclude women from ordained offices in the Church? Isn't that inconsistent?**

First of all, interpreting the Bible literally means to accept *all* the Bible says on a given topic. According to Genesis 1:26-28, God created us in His image—meaning human beings are all inherently equal; and He gave us dominion over the entire animal kingdom— meaning we are inherently free. Slavery came later, after the Fall. Unlike Paul's instructions regarding Church order, which limit the authoritative teaching office of the elder/minister to men, based on the Creation account (1 Tim. 2:11–3:15), nowhere in the Bible is slavery defended as a Creation order. It is of purely human origin. In fact, there are clear biblical prohibitions against selling people into slavery (Exod. 21:16; 1 Tim. 1:10), and Christian slaves were urged to seek their freedom (1 Cor. 7:21). Furthermore, Christians are instructed to treat slaves, in the home and in the Church, with compassion as fellow servants of Christ (1 Cor. 7:22, 23) because, as believers, we are all slaves, with Christ as our one Master (Eph. 6:5–9; Col. 3:22–4:1). In the Lord, then, no one is really a slave, but a sister or a brother (Philem. 16).[23]

3. **Wasn't Paul's instructions to Timothy addressing local problems in the church at Ephesus?**

Paul's epistles to Timothy and Titus are not addressed to specific churches but give instructions to these ministers regarding how to organize churches in the various places where they labored and constitute the inspired directions for Church order and organization.[24] The Adventist pioneers drew heavily from these books, along with other New Testament passages, in establishing the system of Church officers we have today (see the section soon to follow dealing with Adventist history). Paul seems to indicate to Timothy his instructions concerning "godly edification" (NKJV); that is, "good order" (ESV, margin) for the Church (1 Tim. 1:4). In fact, he closes the first main section on Church order and offices by reiterating that the Church should follow similar leadership principles as the home, because it is "the house of God" (3:15).[25]

4. Is it a principle of Seventh-day Adventist interpretation that the Bible should always be understood literally?

Almost always, but not always. There are some exceptions to this general rule. Fortunately, we have inspired guidance as to what those exceptions are, so God has not left us to guess! Ellen White tells us:

> The language of the Bible should be explained according to its *obvious* meaning, *unless a symbol or figure is employed.* Christ has given the promise: "If any man will do His will, he shall know of the doctrine." John 7:17. If men would but *take the Bible as it reads*, if there were no false teachers to mislead and confuse their minds, a work would be accomplished that would make angels glad and that would bring into the fold of Christ thousands upon thousands who are now wandering in error.[26]

Even figures and symbols are not that hard to decipher, because the Bible itself provides the key to unlock their meaning. The problem is that some would have us believe there are many other exceptions based on cultural mores rather than biblical values. There are actually very few examples of this kind in the New Testament—mainly, head coverings (1 Cor. 11:3-16) and the holy kiss (Rom. 16:16)—and even in these cases, the principles underlying the forms (decorum in worship and warmly greeting fellow Christians) still apply. In fact, Western cultural pressures, not cultural prejudices embedded in Scripture, underlie recent questioning of the principle of Creation order male leadership in the home and in the Church.

5. **Why do equally dedicated Adventist theologians who believe the Bible come to opposite conclusions on women's ordination?**

We all come to the Bible with preconceived ideas that may or may not be accurate. It is important for us to be willing to submit these ideas to the standard of God's infallible Word. Ellen White solemnly warns: "If the professed followers of Christ would accept God's standard, it would bring them into unity; but so long as human wisdom is exalted above His Holy Word, there will be divisions and dissension."[27] God's Word will interpret itself if we allow it to do so. "The Bible is clear upon all points which relate to Christian duty,"[28] she said, and "the Scriptures are plain upon the relations and rights of men and women."[29] For a more detailed explanation, see Chapter 1, "Same Book—Different Answers?"

6. **Do the Bible writers sometimes use the masculine gender to refer to both men and women?**

When addressing groups of people, both men and women, Bible writers typically use masculine terms of address: "men of Galilee" (Acts 1:11), "brethren" (Acts 1:16; Rom. 1:13; 7:1; 8:12), "men of Israel" (Acts 2:22), etc. Similarly, commands in the Old Testament, such as the Ten Commandments, use a masculine form as the "default gender" even though it is addressed to everyone. Commands in the New Testament, however, are normally gender-neutral (e.g., Matt. 5:21, 27; 19:18, 19; Rom. 7:7). When it was important to make a distinction in gender, the writers did so.

7. **How can we know if the Bible writers meant the masculine gender to mean only men and not to include women?**

When the biblical writers needed to be more specific, it was not a problem to refer to men only or women only. In guidelines on Christian behavior in the home, both Peter and Paul refer separately to husbands and wives (1 Pet. 3:1-7; Eph. 5:22, 33). In 1 Timothy, Paul deals in turn with matters that concern everyone (2:1-6, prayer is to be offered for all people, God desires all people to be saved, Christ died for all), then how men and women should relate in the worship setting (2:8-15, men are to lead in worship and prayer, women should dress modestly and not usurp the teaching authority of the minister/elder), and, finally, qualifications for Church officers (3:1-12). The minister/elder who oversees the Church is to be "the husband of one wife" (1 Tim. 3:2). Of sixty-one translations surveyed, all but four use wording in this verse to indicate that the person had to be male (see Appendix 2, "English Bible Translations of 1 Timothy 3:2"). The word for "husband" (*anēr*) is never used by Paul generically in the sense of "person" and here it is impossible to understand it that way because the elder must have a wife. Had Paul wanted to allow for women as elders, he could have simply said the elder should be "the husband of one wife or the wife of one husband" (he uses the latter phrase in 1 Tim. 5:9). For a more detailed explanation, see Chapter 4, "The Husband of One Wife . . . Really?" and Appendix 6, "Theology of Ordination: Position No. 1."

8. If there is nothing in the Bible against ordaining women, then why can't they be ordained to the gospel ministry?

Arguments from silence are not strong. For example, there are many things that the Bible doesn't specifically prohibit, such as smoking, but just because it isn't specifically prohibited doesn't mean it's acceptable. In such cases, it is important to look at the bigger picture—the larger principles in the Bible that might apply to the subject in question. Furthermore, the Bible is not silent on the issue, because Paul indicates to both Timothy and Titus that one of the qualifications for being ordained to the office of minister/elder who oversees the Church is that the person "*must be . . .* the husband of one wife" (1 Tim. 3:2; similarly, Titus 1:6).

9. If we interpret the Bible to allow women to be ordained, doesn't that open the door to interpret the Bible any way we want?

While some assure us that this will not happen, it is very difficult to see what is to prevent further fogging of biblical principles when they come into collision with Western cultural biases. Not so long ago it was widely accepted, even among the vast majority of Adventist scholars, that the biblical requirement of the minister/elder being "the husband of one wife" was unequivocally calling for men to serve in this office. If we can now understand this phrase to mean "wife of one husband" or simply "faithful man or woman," then we can make any text of Scripture mean whatever we want. For example, a growing number of evangelical scholars, who supposedly hold to a high view of Scripture, reject the idea that Romans 1:26-28 constitutes a blanket condemnation of lesbianism and homosexuality, preferring to read it as a reference either to non-consensual sex or multiple sexual partners. Thus they seek to carve out space for monogamous same-sex relationships. Even some Adventists are now prepared to argue along similar lines.

Theological Questions Concerning the Old Testament

Before the Entrance of Sin

1. **Does the fact that man was created first and then woman indicate a difference in terms of Church leadership?**

In the Creation account, Adam and Eve are the prototypical man and woman who are given dominion over the fish, the birds, and the land animals (Gen. 1:26, 28). They are also the ideal husband and wife, married by God Himself (Gen. 2:24; Matt. 19:4-6). Genesis 2 describes their individual creation. God did not make two Adams, nor did He create Adam and Eve at the same time or in the same way. As the prototypical man, Adam was given specific responsibilities before Eve was created—including the task of describing Eve in relation to himself (Gen. 2:23): as "woman" (Heb. *'isha*), who came from "man" (Heb. *'ish*). When God judged the pair, He approached and questioned Adam first, despite the fact that Eve had sinned first. Adam, not Eve, is responsible for plunging the human race into sin and death (Rom. 5:12). This illustrates the principle of Creation order male leadership that Paul refers to in connection with both the home (Eph. 5:31, quoting Gen. 2:24) and the Church (1 Cor. 11:8, 9 and 1 Tim. 2:13, both referring to Gen. 2).

2. Does the fact that woman was created from man mean that she is inferior to man in any way?

Not at all. Genesis 1 describes the creation of the first human beings in these words: "God created man in His own image, in the image of God He created him; male and female He created them" (Gen. 1:27). Since both man and woman are created in God's image, both have equal value. Modern culture wants us to think that equal means identical. But equality does not destroy our uniqueness. Adam and Eve were alike in the ability to think and reason but different in temperament and body. They were also created by God at different times and with different roles. The man was to "keep the garden," (Gen. 2:15) and was told what to eat and what to avoid (Gen. 2:16, 17); the woman was given as man's "helper" (Gen. 2:18). Eve shares with Adam the divine dominion (Gen. 1:26), and he can't lead without her because she is his helper (Gen. 2:18, 20). Paul's reasoning in 1 Timothy 2 and 3 takes us back to this foundational leadership principle based on the Creation order: "Adam was formed first, then Eve" (vs. 13). By mentioning the Creation order, man first and then woman, Paul brings us back to Eden and shows that its ideal leadership arrangement is valid in the Church for all time.

3. Were Adam and Eve priests in an Eden "sanctuary"?

The suggestion, now gaining popularity among some Adventists, that Eden is a sanctuary, is more compatible with critical biblical scholarship, which claims that the Eden narrative was actually written much later and betrays signs of an idealized wilderness sanctuary being retrojected back into the Genesis Creation account. There is no strong evidence for the Garden of Eden being a sanctuary, other than the fact that God visited it and conversed with Adam and Eve there. The Hebrew words used to show an "intertextual" connection between Genesis 2 and the later sanctuary (*'abad*, "tend," and *shamar*, "keep") are some of the most common words in the Hebrew Bible, occurring literally hundreds of times, and have different meanings when applied to the wilderness sanctuary. Other supposed connections are likewise more imagined than real.[30] Rather than Eden being a sanctuary, we are told that it was given them as their home and that it "was to be a pattern for other homes as their children should go forth to occupy the earth."[31]

After the Entrance of Sin

1. **Is God's verdict that man would "rule" over the woman the model for leadership in the home and in the Church?**

God's model for leadership is never to "rule" over anyone in the sense of absolute power. To the contrary, the Creation order model for leadership is based on love and unselfish service for the good of others. Sadly, after sin entered this world, relationship dynamics changed, and it became the human tendency to "rule," which is essentially what enticed Eve to eat the fruit in the first place, to "be like God" (Gen. 3:5).[32] The Hebrew word translated "rule" has, in these early chapters of Genesis, a positive connotation. It refers to the rule of the sun and moon over the day and night (1:18) and to the desirability of Cain to rule over sin, which wanted to control him (4:7). This latter instance suggests a power struggle that may exist in human relations too (see Gen. 37:8). In order to understand what the nature of this "rule" of the man over the woman should be like, we need to look more broadly at the biblical principles of servant leadership, which apply within the home as well as the church (e.g., Eph. 5:22-33).

2. **Are women prevented from leadership in the home and in the Church because Eve was deceived and Adam wasn't?**

No. The model of male leadership for both the home (Eph. 5:31-33) and the Church (1 Tim. 2:12, 13) was established as part of the Creation order (Gen. 2), before the entrance of sin. Paul refers to Eve's deception by the serpent, because her acting independently of Adam's leadership role made her more susceptible to being deceived (1 Tim. 2:14). The apostle understands the dramatic leadership shift reflected in the accounts of the Creation and the Fall. In

Genesis 2, God creates Adam first (vs. 7) and gives him the leading role (vss. 15-23: tending the garden, receiving instruction regarding what may and may not be eaten, naming the animals, and describing who Eve is in terms of himself). When we come to Genesis 3, the order is reversed: serpent-Eve-Adam-God. Eve is deceived into thinking that she is in charge: approaching the forbidden tree; parleying with the serpent there; restating (inaccurately) God's command about what may and may not be eaten; deciding on her own that the tree was, in fact, "good for food," "pleasant to the eyes," and "desirable to make one wise"; taking the fruit; eating it; giving the fruit to her husband to eat. Adam, in accepting the fruit from Eve not only disobeyed God's command by eating it but accepted her lead, plunging the race into sin. That is why the "investigative judgment" starts with Adam and why God's verdict begins with the words, "Because you have heeded the voice of your wife . . ." (Gen. 3:17).

3. Does Deborah's judging Israel set an example for positive female leadership in the Church?

Without question, Deborah was an exemplary woman of sterling character. She also had tremendous influence, not the least because she was a prophetess and, in the absence of strong male leadership, people resorted to her for judgment. Although Barak had been designated by the Lord as the one to deliver Israel, he was slow to take the lead.[33] The time of the Judges was far from an ideal time in Israel's history, and the text indicates the exceptional nature of Deborah's leadership in several ways: she is never called a judge, the typical formula for judges ("X" judged Israel "Y" years) is never used of her; in fact, the period of her judging seems to be quite brief ("at that time," Judg. 4:4) and in an unusual location ("under the palm tree," vs. 5, rather than "in the gate," where judgments were normally rendered). Deborah does not constitute a precedent for female leadership in the Church because her primary religious role was as a prophetess, not a priest. Like other prophetesses (and prophets) throughout Scripture who were chosen independently of the leadership structure that existed in Israel and in the Church, Deborah was called and appointed directly by the Lord Himself.

Theological Questions Concerning the New Testament

1. What roles did women have in connection with the ministry of Jesus?

Women played very important supportive roles in the ministry of Jesus, including giving financial support, encouragement, and being His witnesses. Mary, the sister of Martha, sat at Jesus' feet as a disciple. Women who supported Him financially include "Joanna the wife of Chuza, Herod's steward, and Susanna, and many others who provided for Him from their substance" (Luke 8:3). Mary Magdalene was present at the crucifixion, together with other women, including another Mary and Salome, who followed Jesus and ministered to Him when He was in Galilee (Mark 15:40, 41). These women bought spices and went to the tomb early on Sunday morning to anoint Jesus' body but found the tomb empty. An angel commanded them to tell the disciples that Jesus had risen from the dead and would meet them in Galilee. According to Matthew, the women saw Jesus, who commanded them to tell the disciples that He was alive (Matt. 28:9, 10). It is significant that Jesus appeared to them, even before the apostles, making these believing women the first witnesses of His resurrection. The fact that the resurrected Jesus appeared first to women followers was amazing, because people in Roman times did not consider the testimony of women reliable. These facts show us that Jesus did not hesitate to challenge Jewish social, cultural, and educational structures, when it was important to do so.

2. Did Jesus choose only men as apostles for cultural reasons?

The fact that the first witnesses of the resurrection were female was contrary to cultural conventions. Nevertheless, Jesus instructed them to tell the others of His resurrection and of the meeting in Galilee (Matt. 28:10). Also, contrary to what was considered acceptable in Jewish culture, Jesus permitted women to follow Him as disciples (Luke 8:2, 3; 10:39, 42), so culture would not seem to be a hindrance to including at least one of these women among the twelve apostles.

Although the reason for Jesus' choice of the twelve is not explicit in Scripture, the Gospel of John and the Book of Acts suggest that it had to do partly with the fact that these men were among His earliest followers (Acts 1:21, 22). This shows that their interest was more spiritual than material, evidenced by their listening to and believing the testimony of John the Baptist about Jesus (John 1:35-51), and their following Jesus before His many miracles made Him famous. Their spiritual commitment is shown also by their staying with Him even after many left off from following Him (John 6:66-69). Women began following Jesus somewhat later, and none of those present in the upper room were nominated as the replacement for Judas Iscariot (Acts 1:21-23), although there were women present who seemingly could have capably filled this position (vs. 14).

3. What roles did women have in connection with Paul's ministry?

We have ample evidence that in the New Testament Church women worked in various capacities within local congregations. For example, Priscilla and her husband Aquila, who in their spare time worked with Paul in Corinth, Ephesus, and Rome, taught accurately "the way of God" (Acts 18:26). In addition, Aquila and Priscilla opened their home for church gatherings (1 Cor. 16:9; Rom. 16:3-5). Mary of Jerusalem (mother of John Mark) and Lydia of Philippi are also mentioned as hosting Christian gatherings (see Acts 12:12; 16:15). In Romans 16, Paul gives greetings to a long list of believers, including many women who were actively helping in the work of the Lord (see also Chapter 3, "Some Notable Women in the Bible," and the discussion in this chapter of Rom. 16).

4. If women must keep silent in church (1 Cor. 14:34) shouldn't they be excluded from preaching and even teaching in Sabbath School?

Unfortunately, 1 Corinthians 14 is one of the most misunderstood passages of the New Testament. Looking at the passage in its entirety reveals that this chapter addresses the practices of three groups who were causing significant disruptions in the worship service at Corinth—and they were caused *by men as well as women:* (a) men were speaking in tongues without an interpreter (vss. 27, 28); (b) men were prophesying without interpretation (vss. 29-33); (c) women "kept asking questions" while people were speaking (vss. 34, 35). Paul commands *all three groups* (including the men who were being disruptive) to "keep silent." We need to remember that Paul isn't talking about a Sabbath School class, but is explaining how the Christians in Corinth could preserve reverence and decorum in the worship service.

If in your church today men and women were being as disruptive as they were at the church in Corinth, of course they would be told to be silent and stop disrupting the service. It doesn't mean that they must forever remain silent, but that they should speak in Christian love and orderliness. In fact, Paul permits women to pray and prophesy, as long as they exhibit reverence in the worship service and show respect for Creation order male leadership by dressing modestly (1 Cor. 11:3-5, 8, 9). For more on this question, see Chapter 5, "Must Women Keep Silent?"

Questions About Ellen White

1. Was Ellen White ever ordained?

According to the Trustees of the Ellen G. White Estate, Ellen White "was never ordained by human hands, nor did she ever perform a wedding, organize a church, or conduct a baptism."[34] Ellen White was called by God to be His prophetic messenger in the last days, but she was never ordained as a gospel minister, and there is no record of any ordination service held for her.

2. Was Ellen White given credentials as an ordained minister?

Since the Church, of course, doesn't issue credentials for prophets, beginning in 1871 until her death, the General Conference issued to Ellen White the highest credentials in existence—those granted to ordained ministers—as a practical way of granting her full access to pulpits worldwide. On her credentials issued in 1885, the word *ordained* is neatly struck out. To see a picture of Ellen White's credentials and to read more on this specific question, see Chapter 7, "But What About Ellen White?"

3. Doesn't Ellen White say that both men and women should be "pastors to the flock of God"?

Yes, Ellen White does say that,[35] but we need to keep in mind how she used the term *pastors*. During her lifetime, the Adventist Church employed virtually no "settled pastors" having as their primary responsibility oversight of a local church, because that was the role of the elder/overseer, as described in the New Testament (Acts 14:23; Phil. 1:1; Titus 1:5). By "pastors," here and in other places, Ellen White refers to those who have the gift of pastoring or shepherding, visiting church members, and nurturing the "flock." Her normal term for what we would today call "pastor" is "minister," which occurs thousands of times in her writings, whereas "pastor" is far less frequently used by her and, as already indicated, has a different nuance. For a much more detailed discussion of this statement and related issues, see Chapter 7, "But What About Ellen White?"

4. Doesn't Ellen White support women being ordained to ministry by the laying on of hands?

The phrase "laying on of hands" doesn't always mean being ordained to the gospel ministry. Ellen White mentions the Jewish use of this ritual for the blessing of children and devoting animals for sacrifice.[36] When writing about physicians, she wrote, "The work of the true medical missionary is largely a spiritual work. It includes prayer and the laying on of hands."[37] Clearly, this use of the phrase refers to the laying on of hands for those who are sick, rather than ordination. Ellen White wrote in 1895: "Women who are willing to consecrate some of their time to the service of the Lord should be appointed to visit the sick, look after the young, and minister to the necessities of the poor. They should be set apart to this work by prayer and laying on of hands. In some cases they will need to counsel with the church officers or the minister, but if they are devoted women, maintaining a vital connection with God, they will be a power for good in the church."[38] Notice that these women who work only part time, are is to "counsel with the church officers or the minister"—indicating that they are not ministers or even church officers but may still be set aside to do the important work of visiting the sick, looking after the young and ministering to the poor.

5. **Did Ellen White suggest we needed more light on the role of women in the Church?**

This question refers to a 1909 statement of Ellen White written to A. G. Daniells, the General Conference president: "Study the Scriptures for further light on this point. Women were among Christ's devoted followers in the days of His ministry, and Paul makes mention of certain women who were helpers together with him in the gospel."[39] A consideration of the context of this statement shows that Ellen White is encouraging remuneration for wives who labor effectively alongside their husbands in the ministry ("Elder Haskell and his wife") as well as in medical missionary work ("Dr. Kress and his wife"). Both women were clearly devoting significant time and effort and having substantial success, more so it seems than if they were not part of a team ministry: "Brother and Sister Kress can accomplish more than if they labored separately."[40] The principle being expressed is that more than our publications are needed to spread the message of truth—consecrated people are needed too:

> If necessary, let us limit the number of our periodical publications, and let us send forth men and women to labor in faith and consecration for the giving of this last message of mercy to the world. When it is possible let the minister and his wife go forth together. The wife can often labor by the side of her husband, accomplishing a noble work. She can visit the homes of the people and help the women in these families in a way that her husband cannot.[41]

Additional counsels of Ellen White, that describe the positive contributions women can and should make to the Lord's work, are described in Chapter 8, "A 'Woman Ministry.'"

Questions About Seventh-day Adventist Church History

1. Isn't ordination something Adventists inherited from other Churches?

No. Our Adventist pioneers demanded a plain "Thus saith the Lord" for everything they believed and practiced.[42] After two key visions of Ellen White about "Bible Order" in 1850 and 1852,[43] James White and others studied the subject of Church order and gospel ministry from the Bible, establishing an organization at the local church level that remained virtually unchanged until the 1970s.[44] Furthermore, Adventists have always considered the ordination of gospel ministers to transcend national and cultural boundaries, because our message and mission is worldwide (Matt. 28:18-20; Rev. 14:6), based on the eternal Word of God which transcends these boundaries (Isa. 40:8).

2. Did the pioneers expect to find in Scripture the answer to every question?

Our pioneers gleaned from the Bible all the information possible about every matter of faith and practice. The system of local church officers (minister/elder, deacon) had been carefully studied out from diligent Bible study in the 1850s. However, as James White explained in 1859, the Bible doesn't directly address every single issue that might arise, such as whether to have yearly meetings, a weekly paper, or a printing press, and so "we should not be afraid of that system which is not opposed by the Bible, and is approved by sound sense."[45] He wasn't suggesting that in these areas the Bible need not be consulted. Principles are to be gleaned from Scripture to guide us in areas not directly addressed there, as we have done; for example, in establishing our system of freewill offerings, dealing with lifestyle issues (smoking, drug abuse, gambling), etc. Rather than inventing a new method of biblical interpretation or changing the system of organization they had worked out from Scripture, James White suggested *building upon* the biblical order already established.

3. What roles did women fill in the first hundred years of Adventist Church history?

From the very beginning of the Advent movement, women played vital roles in the formation, growth, and nurture of the Church. Ellen G. White was not merely one of our Church founders, she was an inspired messenger of the Lord. Through her prophetic gift, she gave direction and guidance to the Church for seventy years during her lifetime and, through her writings, continues to speak to the Church today. Rachel Oakes, a Seventh Day Baptist, introduced the seventh-day Sabbath to our early Adventist pioneers. As a gifted speaker, Sarah Lindsay worked effectively alongside her minister husband, greatly increasing their effectiveness. Many other ministers' wives contributed greatly to the work, such as "Mrs. Starr, Haskell, Wilson and Robinson—who have been devoted, earnest, whole-souled workers, giving Bible readings and praying with families, helping along by personal efforts just as successfully as their husbands," wrote Ellen White.[46] Prior to the 1930s, women held some of the highest positions of leadership in the Church. Three were treasurers of the General Conference, many served as editor or co-editor of *The Youth's Instructor*. A number of women also served as secretary (director) of various General Conference departments or Church associations.[47]

4. Why has the church at three separate General Conference sessions refused to ordain women?

The General Conference in session has repeatedly refused to ordain women because the vast majority of Seventh-day Adventists do not believe that the practice is biblical. In 1881, when the resolution to ordain women was brought to the floor of the GC Session, it was referred to the General Conference Committee, which was a polite way of rejecting the resolution.[48] In 1990, the GC session decided overwhelmingly (by a vote of 1,173 to only 377 against,[49]) *not* to ordain women. At the 1995 GC session, the North American Division brought forward a request that "where circumstances do not render it inadvisable, a division may authorize the ordination of qualified individuals without regard to gender." Again, the vote was overwhelmingly against the proposal to allow a division to move forward in ordaining women contrary to the practice of the world church, with only 673 in favor and 1,481 against.[50]

Questions About Practical Issues

1. **Has women's ordination helped other denominations grow?**

We would like to see evidence for this but have seen none. The Adventist Church has an advantage over many other denominations in that we can learn from the recent history of women's ordination in other denominations. Their experience has been almost entirely negative. Generally, it has led not to growth and greater prosperity, but to increased conflict and disunity. In actual fact, schism has followed in the wake of ordaining women, as the experience of the Episcopal and the Presbyterian churches in the United States shows.[51] In many other denominations, the result of ordaining women has been "substantial tension and schism," not greater unity.[52]

2. **Is women's ordination serious enough to split the Church over?**

No. The bigger issue here is the authority of Scripture—does the Bible mean what it says that the minister/elder is to be "the husband of one wife"? If we can take this passage (which is quite clear in the original Greek, as it is in English, and in other languages), to mean what it does not say, then we can take any Bible passage and place whatever meaning on it that we think is most appropriate based on our own understanding and culture. But Christ and His Word are the rock and foundation of the Church, and as long as we are faithful to Him and His will, as revealed in His Word, the Church will not split, though some may leave—as has happened before in our history. On the other hand, once we depart from making His Word the source of all our doctrines and practices, we will have abandoned our biblical foundation, thereby running an even greater risk of splitting the Church, as many other Protestant Churches have painfully discovered.

3. Why does the Church ordain women as elders and yet refuse to ordain the women it hires as pastors?

Unfortunately, the current practice of the Adventist Church is inconsistent. Why women, who are commissioned as ministers and ordained as local elders, are able to perform substantially the same functions as ordained ministers and yet not be ordained does seem to be arbitrary and discriminatory. At the same time, it is indisputable that this policy has arisen more from pragmatic considerations than any biblical mandate. Up to the present time, Adventists have largely remained unconvinced that there is biblical authority for ordaining women to the gospel ministry.

4. Wouldn't allowing ordination to the gospel ministry to be regional rather than worldwide preserve the unity of the Church?

Why should we expect that unity would be preserved by taking additional steps in the direction of ordaining women when the exact opposite has been the case? Over the past forty years, some segments of the Church (still a small fraction of the overall membership) have become increasingly divided and polarized on this issue. Yet, we know of no scientific study that suggests Adventist members in North America largely support ordaining women as ministers. The data that does exist actually seems to point in the opposite direction.[53] Even in divisions where top leadership is supportive of ordaining women, it is difficult to find churches outside of institutional settings that are willing to accept a woman as their senior pastor. The reason there are not more women pastors in these places is not so much that conference presidents are unwilling to hire them but that they have very few options when it comes to placing them in a church setting. For more, see Appendix 7.

5. **If we ordain individuals without regard to gender, would that open the door to gay and transgender individuals being ordained as pastors?**

While, as Adventists, we look to the Bible, not to culture or to other denominations to understand God's will for us, we should not close our eyes to reality! We have a great advantage in being able to learn from the experience of other churches who have traveled this path before us. We do not have to wonder where that path leads. It inevitably begins with a shift in how the Bible is interpreted and how its authority is viewed. It is a well-recognized fact that denominations taking the step to ordain gay and transgender individuals took the step to ordain women first. Examples include many Anglican churches, the Disciples of Christ Church, the Episcopal Church, the Evangelical Lutheran Church, the Presbyterian Church USA, the Universalist Association, United Church of Canada, and the United Church of Christ. It would be naïve and arrogant for Adventists to presume that we would not follow the same path as these other Churches if we vote to ordain individuals without regard to gender.

6. **Doesn't culture play a major role as to whether or not women should be ordained?**

Culture today—especially Western culture—places a high value on equality, fairness, and respecting people's "rights." This has had a positive impact in a number of ways, such as abolishing slavery, allowing women and minorities to vote, equal employment opportunities, and equal pay for equal work. But when we try to use the same mentality and methods that come from a secular setting and apply them to a sacred setting, we can end up with confusion and conflict. No one, whether male or female, has a "right" to be ordained, because it is not ours to give. It is God who has specified the qualifications for ordination in His Word. Yet how often do we hear cries of "discrimination" if women are not allowed "equal access" to the same ministry opportunities as males. The impression is given that young people are leaving the Church because of the "unfairness" of not allowing women to be ordained. But where is the evidence for this? Clearly, the values of fairness and non-discrimination has played a strong role in the thinking of those advocating for women's ordination—not only in the Adventist Church, but in many other denominations as well. Even the secular world around us recognizes the fact that no Church has extended rights to gays and lesbians without first extending ordination to women.[54]

7. What do we say to women who feel called by God to full-time gospel ministry?

The best way to serve God and fulfill His calling is to accept His will as revealed through the Bible and the writings of Ellen White. Women have been given an important and high calling to serve God in a variety of ways, as Chapter 8, "A 'Woman Ministry,'" explains. One of the best examples mentioned there of a woman called by God is S. M. I. Henry, who did a tremendous work for the Lord, spoke to thousands of people, published numerous books, wrote regularly for the *Review*, and ministered to many, especially women, in order to teach them how they could be effective in their families, with their children, and in home-visitation ministry. Though never ordained and never thinking she needed it, she became one of the most prominent Seventh-day Adventists of the late nineteenth century.

8. Haven't we gone too far to turn back now? Wouldn't that inevitably divide the Church?

No. The source of our unity is not political or ecclesiastical. It is rooted in our faith in and faithfulness to God and His Word. The surest way to divide us is to leave that foundation as other Churches have done. Protestantism, as a result, is fractured and fragmented beyond repair. Even a strong, centralized ecclesiastical authority has not prevented significant divisions within the Roman Catholic Church.

While probation lasts, it is never too late to return to God's will for us, as individuals and as a church (2 Cor. 6:16-18). The fact is that the largest Protestant Church in the United States, the Southern Baptist Convention, reversed its course and ceased ordaining women in 1984—with positive results. Other denominations have done the same, including the Presbyterian Church of Australia and the Christian Reformed Church in America (both in 1992). Returning to a biblical basis for our practice in this area would make the Seventh-day Adventist Church stronger and more unified than ever, not weaker.

Endnotes:

1. The vote was 280 to 3 in favor of the document with 4 abstentions. See Andrew McChesney, "Women's Ordination Goes to San Antonio," *Adventist Review*, November 20, 2014, 19.

2. See "Consensus Statement on a Seventh-day Adventist Theology of Ordination" (emphasis original), https://www.adventistarchives.org/consensus-statement-on-a-seventh-day-adventist-theology-of-ordination.pdf (accessed March 17, 2015).

3. See the story of William Hunter in Ted N. C. Wilson, "The Privilege of an Open Bible: Let's be careful to preserve it," *Adventist World*, November 2014, p. 8, http://www.adventistworld.org/images/issues/2014/november/1014-1011.pdf (accessed March 18, 2015).

4. "28 Fundamental Beliefs," http://www.adventist.org/fileadmin/adventist.org/files/articles/official-statements/28Beliefs-Web.pdf (accessed April 1, 2015).

5. Arthur N. Patrick, "The Ordination of Deaconesses," *Adventist Review*, January 16, 1986, 18, 19, refers to ordination services in the Ashfield church held in 1895 and 1900.

6. Ellen G. White, *The Seventh-day Adventist Bible Commentary* (ed. Francis D. Nichol; 7 vols.; Washington, D.C.: Review and Herald, 1956), vol. 5, 1129, par. 3: "But although Christ's divine glory was for a time veiled and eclipsed by His assuming humanity, yet He did not cease to be God when He became man. The human did not take the place of the divine, nor the divine of the human."

7. Roxanne Lalonde, "Unity in Diversity: Acceptance and Integration in an Era of Intolerance and Fragmentation" (edited extract of

M.A. thesis, Carleton University, 1994), http://bahai-library.com/lalonde_unity_diversity, (accessed March 23, 2015).

8. Ellen G. White, *Gospel Workers* (Battle Creek, MI: Review and Herald, 1892), 391.

9. Ellen G. White, in *Historical Sketches of the Foreign Missions of the Seventh-day Adventists* (Basil: Imprimerie Polyglotte, 1886), 197.

10. This section addresses the principal passages used to support the ordination of women to the gospel ministry in Martin Hanna and Cindy Tutsch, eds., *Questions and Answers About Women's Ordination* (Nampa, ID: Pacific Press, 2014), 29-69. Rather than presenting a positive case, it would appear that more space in this portion of their book is devoted to explaining what numerous other passages *cannot* mean.

11. Ellen G. White, *Counsels to Parents, Teachers, and Students* (Mountain View, CA: Pacific Press, 1943), 33.

12. Ellen G. White, "The Marriage in Galilee," *Bible Echo*, August 28, 1899, par. 1.

13. Ellen G. White, *Fundamentals of Christian Education* (Nashville, TN: Southern Publishing Association, 1923), 38.

14. Ellen G. White, *Patriarchs and Prophets* (Mountain View, CA: Pacific Press, 1958), 48.

15. Ibid., 58, 59.

16. The one exception to this rule (which is not really an exception) is the use of ʾadam without the article before the creation of Adam to indicate that "there was no man to till the ground" (Gen. 2:5).

17. The ESV, NAS95, NKJV, RSV, and NIV11 all use "man" or "mankind" to indicate this clear distinction made by the Hebrew text, while the NRSV prefers "humankind." The Hebrew term *toledot* regularly introduces genealogies of the patriarchs (Gen. 6:9; 10:1; 11:10, 27, etc.).

18. Further, see Edwin Reynolds and Clinton Wahlen, "Minority Report," in *North American Division Theology of Ordination Study Committee Report* (November 2013), 197-200, http://static.squarespace.com/static/50d0ebebe4b0ceb6af5fdd33/t/527970c2e-

4b039a2e8329354/1383690434980/nad-ordination-14-minority. pdf (March 19, 2015).

19. The statement appears in Ellen G. White, *Daughters of God* (Hagerstown, MD: Review and Herald, 2005), 249 (Appendix C).

20. E.g., CEB, NASB, ESV, HCSB, WEB. See the use of *diakonos* as "servant" in the following passages: Matt. 20:26; 23:11; Mark 9:35; 10:43; John 12:26; Rom. 15:8; 1 Cor. 3:5; 2 Cor. 3:6; 6:4; 11:5, 23; Eph. 3:7; 6:21; Col. 1:7, 23, 25; 4:7; 1 Tim. 4:6. Note also that Phoebe is referred to as a "servant" not a deaconess in Ellen G. White, *Testimonies for the Church*, 9 vols. (Mountain View, CA: Pacific Press, 1948), vol. 6, 343, 344.

21. For a more detailed discussion of Rom. 16:7, see Richard Sabuin, "Were Andronicus and Iounian apostles?" *Ministry*, May 2014, 10-13.

22. See Reynolds and Wahlen, "Minority Report," 205, 206.

23. See Benjamin Reaoch, *Women, Slaves, and the Gender Debate: A Complementarian Response to the Redemptive-Movement Hermeneutic* (Phillipsburg, NJ: P&R, 2012).

24. Francis D. Nichol, ed., *The Seventh-day Adventist Bible Commentary*, vol. 6, 107.

25. For a more detailed discussion of this question, see Clinton Wahlen, "Is 'Husband of One Wife' in 1 Timothy 3:2 Gender-Specific?" (paper presented at the Theology of Ordination Study Committee, Columbia, Md., January 23, 2014), 32, 33, https://www.adventistarchives.org/is-"husband-of-one-1-wife"-in-1-timothy-32-gender-specific.pdf (accessed March 18, 2015).

26. Ellen G. White, *The Great Controversy* (Mountain View, CA: Pacific Press, 1950), 598 (emphasis supplied).

27. White, *Patriarchs and Prophets*, 124.

28. White, *Testimonies*, vol. 4, 435.

29. Ibid., vol. 1, 421.

30. See Gerhard Pfandl, "Evaluation of Egalitarian Papers" (paper presented at the Theology of Ordination Study Committee, Colum-

bia, Md., January 2014), 4-6, https://www.adventistarchives.org/evaluation-of-egalitarian-papers.pdf (accessed April 1, 2015).

31. White, *Patriarchs and Prophets*, 47, 49.

32. See Ellen G. White, *Confrontation* (Washington, D.C.: Review and Herald, 1971), 13, 14.

33. For more details about Barak and Deborah, see White, *Daughters of God*, 37-39.

34. The statement appears in Appendix C of White, *Daughters of God*, 249.

35. Ellen G. White, "Canvassers as Gospel Evangelists," *Advent Review and Sabbath Herald*, January 15, 1901, par. 5.

36. Ellen G. White, *The Acts of the Apostles* (Mountain View, CA: Pacific Press, 1911), 162.

37. Ellen G. White, Ms. 5, 1908, in *Manuscript Releases*, 21 vols. (Washington, D.C. and Hagerstown, MD: Review and Herald, 1981-1993), vol. 20, 264.

38. Ellen G. White, "The Duty of the Minister and the People," *The Advent Review and Sabbath Herald*, July 9, 1895, par. 8.

39. White, Letter 142, 1909, in *Manuscript Releases*, vol. 12, 167.

40. Ibid.

41. Ibid., 166.

42. See White, *The Great Controversy*, 595.

43. White, Ms. 11, 1850, in *Manuscript Releases*, vol. 5, 203, 204; Idem, *Early Writings* (Washington, D.C.: Review and Herald, 1945), 97-104.

44. E.g., James White, "Gospel Order," *The Advent Review and Sabbath Herald*, Dec. 6, 1853, 173; Idem, "Gospel Order," *The Advent Review and Sabbath Herald*, Dec. 13, 1853, 180; Idem, "Gospel Order," *The Advent Review and Sabbath Herald*, Dec. 20, 1853, 188-190; Joseph Bates, "Church Order," *The Advent Review and Sabbath Herald*, Aug. 29, 1854, 22, 23; J. B. Frisbie, "Church

Order," *The Advent Review and Sabbath Herald*, Dec. 26, 1854, 147, 148.

45. James White, "Yearly Meetings," *The Advent Review and Sabbath Herald*, July 21, 1859, 68, cols. 2, 3 (quotation in col. 2).

46. White, Letter 137, 1898, in *Manuscript Releases*, vol. 21, 360.

47. Patrick Allen, "The Depression and the Role of Women in the Seventh-day Adventist Church," *Adventist Heritage*, vol. 11, no. 2 (Fall 1986), 50; Roger Coon, "Ellen White's View of the Role of Women in the SDA Church," 2, 3, http://text.egwwritings.org/publication.php?pubtype=Book&bookCode=EGWVRWS-DA&pagenumber=1&paragraphReferences=1 (accessed March 16, 2015).

48. David Trim, "The Ordination of Women in Seventh-day Adventist Policy and Practice, Up to 1972," revised and slightly expanded version of the paper presented at the Theology of Ordination Study Committee, July 22, 2013, 16, https://www.adventistarchives.org/the-ordination-of-women-in-seventh-day-adventist-policy-and-practice.pdf (accessed February 27, 2015).

49. "Session Actions," *Adventist Review*, July 13, 1990, 15.

50. "Session Actions," *Adventist Review*, July 11, 1995, 30.

51. See Paula D. Nesbitt, "Women in Other Professions," in *Women and Work: A Handbook*, edited by Paula J. Dubeck and Kathryn Borman (New York, NY: Garland, 1996), 182, 183.

52. James A. Beckford and N. J. Demerath III, eds., *SAGE Handbook of the Sociology of Religion* (London, England: SAGE, 2007), 304.

53. See F. Donald Yost, "An Inquiry into the Role of Women in the SDA Church," rev. with additional data, December, 1977, https://www.adventistarchives.org/an-inquiry-into-the-role-of-women-in-the-sda-church.pdf (accessed April 1, 2015).

54. Elizabeth Dias, "A Change of Heart: Inside the Evangelical War Over Gay Marriage," *Time*, January 26, 2015, 47. According to Russell Moore, president of the Southern Baptist Convention's Ethics and Religious Liberty Commission, "It is not an accident that the women's-liberation movement preceded the gay-liberation movement" (Ibid.).

APPENDICES

Appendix I

Consensus Statement on a Seventh-day Adventist Theology of Ordination

1   TOSC to AAS-EOM+ADCOM+GCDO13AC+13AC+15GCS

2

3   130-13GS CONSENSUS STATEMENT ON A SEVENTH-DAY
4   ADVENTIST THEOLOGY OF ORDINATION

5

6   RECOMMENDED, To adopt the document, "Consensus Statement on a Seventh-day Adventist
7   Theology of Ordination," which reads as follows:

8

9   In a world alienated from God, the Church is composed of those whom God has reconciled
10   to Himself and to each other. Through the saving work of Christ they are united to Him by faith
11   through baptism (Eph 4:4-6), thus becoming a royal priesthood whose mission is to "proclaim
12   the praises of him who called you out of darkness into his marvelous light" (1 Pet 2:9, NKJV).
13   Believers are given the ministry of reconciliation (2 Cor 5:18-20), called and enabled through the
14   power of the Spirit and the gifts He bestows on them to carry out the Gospel Commission
15   (Matt 28:18-20).

16

17   While all believers are called to use their spiritual gifts for ministry, the Scriptures identify
18   certain specific leadership positions that were accompanied by the Church's public endorsement
19   for persons who meet the biblical qualifications (Num 11:16-17; Acts 6:1-6; 13:1-3; 14:23;
20   1 Tim 3:1-12; Titus 1:5-9). Several such endorsements are shown to involve "the laying on of
21   hands." English versions of the Scriptures use the word *ordain* to translate many different Greek
22   and Hebrew words having the basic idea of *select* or *appoint* that describe the placement of these
23   persons in their respective offices. Over the course of Christian history the term *ordination* has
24   acquired meanings beyond what these words originally implied. Against such a backdrop,
25   Seventh-day Adventists understand ordination, in a biblical sense, as the action of the Church in
26   publicly recognizing those whom the Lord has called and equipped for local and global Church
27   ministry.

28

29   Aside from the unique role of the apostles, the New Testament identifies the following
30   categories of ordained leaders: the elder/supervising elder (Acts 14:23; Acts 20:17, 28;
31   1 Tim 3:2-7; 4:14; 2 Tim 4:1-5; 1 Pet 5:1) and the deacon (Phil 1:1; 1 Tim 3:8-10). While most
32   elders and deacons ministered in local settings, some elders were itinerant and supervised greater
33   territory with multiple congregations, which may reflect the ministry of individuals such as
34   Timothy and Titus (1 Tim 1:3-4; Titus 1:5).

35

36   In the act of ordination, the Church confers representative authority upon individuals for
37   the specific work of ministry to which they are appointed (Acts 6:1-3; 13:1-3; 1 Tim 5:17; Titus
38   2:15). These may include representing the Church; proclaiming the gospel; administering the
39   Lord's Supper and baptism; planting and organizing churches; guiding and nurturing members;
40   opposing false teachings; and providing general service to the congregation (cf. Acts 6:3;
41   20:28-29; 1 Tim 3:2, 4-5; 2 Tim 1:13-14; 2:2; 4:5; Titus 1:5, 9). While ordination contributes to
42   Church order, it neither conveys special qualities to the persons ordained nor introduces a kingly
43   hierarchy within the faith community. The biblical examples of ordination include the giving of a
44   charge, the laying on of hands, fasting and prayer, and committing those set apart to the grace of
45   God (Deut 3:28; Acts 6:6; 14:26; 15:40).

46

Contd
Revised 07-23-13tkb

1   Ordained individuals dedicate their talents to the Lord and to His Church for a lifetime of
2   service. The foundational model of ordination is Jesus appointing the twelve apostles
3   (Matt 10:1-4; Mark 3:13-19; Luke 6:12-16), and the ultimate model of Christian ministry is the
4   life and work of our Lord, who came not to be served but to serve (Mark 10:45; Luke 22:25-27;
5   John 13:1-17).

Appendix 2

English Bible Translations of 1 Timothy 3:2

Year	Version Translation	Least Restrictive .... Most Restrictive					
		male or female, married	male, married or single	male, married	male, married, not polygamous emphasized	male, married, faithful	male, married only once
1382	Wycliffe Bible, ©2001 by Terence P. Noble "Therefore it behooveth a bishop to be without reproof [Therefore it behooveth a bishop to be irreprehensible, *or without reproof*], **the husband of one wife**. . . ."			X			
1599	Geneva Bible (GNV) "A Bishop therefore must be unreproveable, **the husband of one wife**. . . ."			X			
1858	Sawyer's New Testament "It is necessary therefore that a bishop should be blameless, **a husband of one wife**. . . ."			X			
1875	Davidson's New Testament "The bishop then must be blameless, **husband of one wife**. . . ."			X			
1884	Revised Version (RV) "The bishop therefore must be without reproach, **the husband of one wife**. . . ."			X			
1890	Darby Translation (DARBY) "The overseer then must be irreproachable, **husband of one wife**. . . ."			X			
1898	Young's Literal Translation (YLT) "it behoveth, therefore, the overseer to be blameless, **of one wife a husband**. . . ."				X		
1899	Douay-Rheims American Edition (DRA) "It behoveth therefore a bishop to be blameless, **the husband of one wife**. . . ."			X			
1900	Authorized Version (KJV), Cambridge "A bishop then must be blameless, **the husband of one wife**. . . ."			X			
1901	American Standard Version (ASV) "The bishop therefore must be without reproach, **the husband of one wife**. . . ."			X			
1902	Weymouth's New Testament in Modern Speech "A minister then must be a man of irreproachable character, **true to his one wife**. . . ."					X	
1903	20th Century New Testament "The Presiding-Officer should be a man of blameless character; **he should have been only once married**. . . ."						X
1937	Williams' New Testament: A Translation in the Language of the People "So the pastor must be a man above reproach, **must have only one wife**. . . ."				X		
1946	Wand's New Testament Letters "A bishop has to be irreproachable, **with only one wife**. . . ."				X		

Year	Version Translation	Least Restrictive .... Most Restrictive					
		male or female, married	male, married or single	male, married	male, married, not polygamous emphasized	male, married, faithful	male, married only once
1954	Goodspeed "A superintendent must be a man above reproach, **only once married. . . .**"						X
1961	New World Translation "The overseer should therefore be irreprehensible, **a husband of one wife. . . .**"			X			
1961	Norley's Simplified New Testament "The pastor should be a man of irreproachable character, and **never have more than one wife. . . .**"				X		
1963	Holy Name Bible (HNB) "A bishop then must be blameless, **the husband of one wife. . . .**"			X			
1965	Bruce's The Letters of Paul: An Expanded Paraphrase "The bishop therefore must be without reproach, **the husband of one wife. . . .**"			X			
1966	The Jerusalem Bible (JB) "That is why the president must have an impeccable character, **He must not have been married more than once. . . .**"						X
1969	Barclay "The superintendent of the community must therefore be a man whom no one can criticize. **He must be the faithful husband of one wife. . . .**"					X	
1969	New Berkeley Version (NBV) "The bishop, then, must be above reproach, **the husband of only one wife. . . .**"				X		
1969	New Life Version (NLV) "A church leader must be a good man. His life must be so no one can say anything against him. **He must have only one wife. . . .**"				X		
1970	New American Bible (NAB) "**A bishop must be** irreproachable, **married only once. . . .**"	X					
1971	The Living Bible (LB) "For a pastor must be a good man whose life cannot be spoken against. **He must have only one wife. . . .**"				X		
1971	Revised Standard Version (RSV) "Now a bishop must be above reproach, **the husband of one wife. . . .**"			X			
1972	Phillips' New Testament in Modern English "Well, for the office of a bishop a man must be of blameless reputation, **he must be married to one wife only. . . .**"				X		

Year	Version Translation	Least Restrictive .... Most Restrictive					
		male or female, married	male, married or single	male, married	male, married, not polygamous emphasized	male, married, faithful	male, married only once
1977	New American Standard Bible (NASB) "An overseer, then, must be above reproach, **the husband of one wife.** ..."			X			
1982	New King James Version (NKJV) "A bishop then must be blameless, **the husband of one wife.** ..."			X			
1984	New International Version (NIV) "Now the overseer must be above reproach, **the husband of but one wife.** ..."				X		
1985	New Jerusalem Bible (NJB) "That is why the presiding elder must have an impeccable character. **Husband of one wife.** ..."			X			
1987	Amplified Bible (AMP) "Now a bishop (superintendent, overseer) must give no grounds for accusation *but* must be above reproach, **the husband of one wife.** ..."			X			
1989	New Revised Standard Version (NRSV) "Now **a bishop must be** above reproach, **married only once.** ..."	X					
1989	Revised English Bible (REB) "A bishop, therefore, must be above reproach, **husband of one wife.** ..."			X			
1992	Good News Translation (GNT) "A church leader must be without fault; **he must have only one wife.** ..."				X		
1994	21st Century King James Version (KJ21) "A bishop then must be blameless, **the husband of one wife.** ..."			X			
1995	Contemporary English Version (CEV) "That's why **officials must** have a good reputation and **be faithful in marriage.** ..."	X					
1995	GOD'S WORD Translation (GW) "A bishop must have a good reputation. **He must have only one wife.** ..."				X		
1995	New American Standard Bible (NAS95) "An overseer, then, must be above reproach, **the husband of one wife.** ..."			X			
1998	Complete Jewish Bible (CJB) "A congregation leader must be above reproach, **he must be faithful to his wife.** ..."					X	
1998	New International Reader's Version (NIRV) "A leader must be free from blame. **He must be faithful to his wife.** ..."					X	

Year	Version Translation	Least Restrictive .... Most Restrictive					
		male or female, married	male, married or single	male, married	male, married, not polygamous emphasized	male, married, faithful	male, married only once
1998	Worldwide English (New Testament) (WE) "For a man to be a church leader, people must speak well of him. **He must have only one wife. . . .**"				X		
2000	Jubilee Bible 2000 (JUB) "It is expedient, therefore, that the bishop be blameless, **the husband of only one wife. . . .**"				X		
2000	The Clear Word (CW) "An elder should be someone who is blameless. **If he's married, he should be loyal to his wife.**"		X				
2001	English Standard Version (ESV) "Therefore an overseer must be above reproach, **the husband of one wife. . . .**"			X			
2002	The Message (MSG) "there are preconditions: A leader must be well-thought-of, **committed to his wife. . . .**"					X	
2005	New Century Version (NCV) "An overseer must not give people a reason to criticize him, and **he must have only one wife. . . .**"				X		
2006	Easy-to-Read Version (ERV) "An elder must be such a good man that no one can rightly criticize him. **He must be faithful to his wife. . . .**"					X	
2006	New English Translation (NET) "The overseer then must be above reproach, **the husband of one wife. . . .**"			X			
2007	New Living Translation (NLT) "So an elder must be a man whose life is above reproach. **He must be faithful to his wife. . . .**"					X	
2009	Holman Christian Standard Bible (HCSB) "An overseer, therefore, must be above reproach, **the husband of one wife. . . .**"			X			
2011	Common English Bible (CEB) "So **the church's supervisor** must be without fault. **They should be faithful to their spouse. . . .**"	X					
2011	Expanded Bible (EXB), "An overseer must not give people a reason to criticize him [have a good reputation; be above reproach], and **he must have only one wife** [*or* be faithful to his wife] . . . ."				X	[X]	
2011	Mounce Reverse-Interlinear New Testament (MOUNCE) "Therefore, it is necessary for an overseer to be above reproach: **a man of one woman. . . .**"			X			

Year	Version Translation	Least Restrictive .... Most Restrictive					
		male or female, married	male, married or single	male, married	male, married, not polygamous emphasized	male, married, faithful	male, married only once
2011	Names of God Bible (NOG) "A bishop must have a good reputation. **He must have only one wife. . . .**"				X		
2011	New International Version (NIV11) "Now the overseer is to be above reproach, **faithful to his wife. . . .**"					X	
2011	Orthodox Jewish Bible (OJB) "It is necessary, therefore, for the congregational Mashgiach Ruchani to be without reproach, ba'al isha echat (**a one woman man/master,** *see OJB p.258, 1Sm 2:22-25, i.e., kedushah and tahorah characterized by heterosexuality, exclusivity, and fidelity*) . . . ."					X	
2012	Lexham English Bible (LEB) "Therefore the overseer must be irreproachable, **the husband of one wife. . . .**"			X			
2012	The Voice (VOICE) "*Here are the qualifications to look for in* an overseer: a spotless reputation, **the husband of one wife. . . .**"			X			
N.D.	Free Bible Version "An elder must be above reproach, **married to one wife. . . .**"				X		
N.D.	World English Bible (WEB) "The overseer therefore must be without reproach, **the husband of one wife. . . .**"			X			
Totals		4	1	27	17	9	3

Endnote:

1. This list represents all English translations from the Biblical Research Institute library and on www.biblegateway.com, excluding regional editions of the same translation.

Appendix 3

Similarities Between 1 Timothy and Titus

Author	1:1 – Paul, . . . an apostle of Christ Jesus according to the commandment of God our Savior	1:1, 3 – Paul, an apostle of Jesus Christ . . . by the command of God our Savior
Addressee	1:2 – To Timothy, my true child in the faith; 1:18 – my son	1:4 – To Titus, my true child in a common faith
Purpose	3:15 – I write so that you will know how one ought to conduct himself in the household of God	1:5, 7 – so that you might put what remained into order and appoint elders . . . as God's steward
Qualifications for the Overseer/Elder	3:2 – An overseer, then, must be above reproach, the husband of one wife, temperate, prudent, respectable, hospitable, able to teach,	1:7 – An overseer . . . must be above reproach 1:6 – the husband of one wife 1:8 – self-controlled, . . . disciplined 1:8 – a lover of good 1:8 – upright 1:8 – hospitable 1:7 – He must hold firm to the trustworthy word as taught, so that he may be able to give instruction in sound doctrine and also to rebuke those who contradict it.
	3:3 – not addicted to wine [not] pugnacious, gentle, peaceable, free from the love of money. 3:4 – He must be one who manages his own household well, keeping his children under control with all dignity	1:7 – He must not . . . be a drunkard 1:7 – [not] quick-tempered or . . . violent 1:8 – holy 1:7 – [not] greedy for gain, 1:6 – his children are believers and not open to the charge of debauchery or insubordination
Deceivers	1:3 – Certain men . . . teach strange doctrines 1:4 – myths 1:4 – endless genealogies 1:7 – teachers of the law 1:7 – do not understand . . . what they are saying 1:6 – fruitless discussion 6:20 – empty chatter 6:5 – men of depraved mind 6:5 – who suppose that godliness is a means of gain 6:5 – constant friction	1:10 – deceivers 1:14 – turn away from the truth 1:14 – myths 3:9 – genealogies 3:9 – quarrels about the law 1:10 – empty talkers 3:9 – unprofitable and worthless [quarrels] 1:15 – their minds and their consciences are defiled 1:11 – teaching for shameful gain what they ought not to teach 3:9 – dissensions
Instructions for	5:1 – Older man . . . appeal to as a father, to the younger men as brothers	2:2 - Older men are to be sober-minded, dignified

older/younger men/women	5:2 – the older women as mothers and the younger women as sisters	2:6 – urge the younger men to be self-controlled 2:3 – Older women . . . are to be reverent in behavior 2:4 – young women to love their husbands and children
Instructions for slaves	6:1 – slaves are to regard their own masters as worthy of all honor 6:2 – [they] must not be disrespectful to them	2:9 – Bondservants are to be submissive to their own masters in everything; . . . well-pleasing 2:9-10 – not argumentative, not pilfering, but showing all good faith
Personal Instructions	4:11 – Prescribe and teach these things 4:12 – Let no one look down on your youthfulness 4:12 – In speech, conduct, love, faith and purity, show yourself an example of those who believe 4:16 – Pay close attention to yourself and your teaching	2:15 – Declare these things; exhort and rebuke with all authority. 2:15 – Let no one disregard you 2:7 – Show yourself in all respects to be a model of good works 2:7-8 – in your teaching show integrity, dignity, and sound speech

Appendix 4

Reply on Behalf of W. C. White Regarding Ellen G. White's Credentials

Nov. 17, 1935.

Elder L.E. Froom
Takoma Park, D.C.

Dear Brother Froom:

Elder White has just shown me your letter of Nov. 8, regarding the Ministerial credentials of Mrs. White, and he tells me that Sister White was never ordained, that she never baptized, nor did she ever give the ordination charge to others.

With this information, I reached over to my desk and pulled out a card reading as follows:

"Credentials granted by the Michigan Conference to Ellen G. White." -- Review and Herald, Feb. 14, 1871, p. 69

I think this was the first time she carried ministerial credentials. They were issued to her because of her evident call of the Lord. I do not know just how long before the General Conference put her on their ministerial list. She did not carry ministerial credentials or any other papers prior to this.

I have a number of letters from you recently, some informative and some with inquiries, and I will soon write to you regarding some of these.

Arthur arrived yesterday and gave us a very interesting report of his trip. I assured him that I knew he had a very interesting time with his roommate and he agreed although he said he was too busy to spend much time in visiting.

This noon mail, also brought your letter to him and to me regarding the studies to appear in the Ministry based upon "Gospel Workers." This is something more for us to think about.

This is Friday afternoon so I will not write further.

Sincerely your brother,

DER:lfw.

Appendix 5

Women Licensed as Adventist Ministers
1869-1975[1]

1869		1902	
Mrs. S. A. Lindsay[2]	New York-Pennsylvania	Minnie Syp (later changed to *Sype*)	Oklahoma
1875[3]		**1904**	
Ellen S. Lane	Michigan	Alma Bjdigg	Finland Mission
Roby Tuttle	Michigan	Mrs. J. E. Bond	Arizona
		Bertha E. Jorgensen	South Dakota
1878		**1910**	
Anna Fulton	Minnesota	Pearl Field	Nebraska
Julia Owen	Kentucky-Tennessee	Mrs. Ura Spring	Nebraska
1879		**1920**	
Libbie Collins	Minnesota	Ella H. Osborne	Northern California
Hattie Enoch	Kansas	Emme Wells	Greater New York
Libbie Fulton	Minnesota		
Lizzie Post	Minnesota		
1880		**1925**	
Anna Johnson	Minnesota	Mrs. E. Flo Hawkins	Illinois
		Mrs. B. Miller	East China Union Mission
1881		**1930**	
Ida W. Ballenger	Illinois	Mrs. E. Eder	Northern Texas
Helen L. Morse	Illinois	Mrs. Beulah Langdon	Northern Texas
		Pearl Stafford	Oregon
1884		**1935**	
Ruie Hill	Kansas	Lucy Andrus	Hopei Mission (China)
1886		**1945**	
Ida W. Hibben	Illinois	Jessie Curtis	East Pennsylvania
1887		**1960**	
Mrs. S. E. Pierce	Vermont	Mrs. W. H. Anderson	Central Union Conference
1893			Marye Burdick	Georgia-Cumberland
Flora Plummer	Iowa	Edna J. Cardey	Potomac
1894		Freda Ford	Kentucky-Tennessee
Margaret Caro	New Zealand	Lucia H. Lee	Georgia-Cumberland
1898		Emma Phillips	Kentucky-Tennessee
Mrs. S. M. I. Henry	General Conference	Mary Saxton	Potomac
Lulu Wightman	New York	Mary E. Walsh	Pacific Union
		Mrs. J. W. Wilhelm	Kentucky-Tennessee

1899		1965	
Edith Bartlett	British Conference	Lois Mays	Potomac
		Julia Ross	Potomac
1900		**1970**	
Mrs. Hetty Haskell (wife of S. N. Haskell)	General Conference	Mrs. Phil Neal	Kentucky-Tennessee
Mina Robinson	British Conference	Mrs. Harry Weckham	Kentucky-Tennessee
1901		**1975**	
Carrie V. Hansen	Utah	Josephine Benton	Potomac
Emma Hawkins	Iowa	Clare Yauchzie	Ontario
Mrs. E. R. Williams	Michigan		

Endnotes:

1. Most of this data comes from Appendix D in Roger Coon, "Ellen G. White's View of the Role of Women in the SDA Church," 18 http://egwtext.whiteestate.org/publication.php?pubtype=Book&-bookCode=EGWVRWSDA&lang=en&section=all&pagenumber=18 (February 22, 2015). Some corrections have been made based on William Fagal, "Did Ellen White Support the Ordination of Women?" Ministry 62/2 (February 1989), 7. Upon further checking, Mrs. Sarah A. Lindsay was actually licensed two years earlier than Fagal reports. The table only goes up to 1975 because, for a variety of pragmatic reasons unrelated to Scripture, policies relative to women in ministry changed substantially after that.

2. The license was approved at the final session of the conference, on or about September 16, 1869. See "Report of the N.Y. and Pa. Conference," Review and Herald, Oct 12, 1869, 126.

3. Both women were issued licenses on August 11, 1875. See "Business Proceedings of the Fifteenth Annual Session of the Michigan State Conference," Review and Herald, August 26, 1875, 63.

Appendix 6

Theology of Ordination: Position No. 1

Presented by Clinton Wahlen to the General Conference Executive Committee

October 14, 2014

Introduction

Good morning!

I have good news for us this morning: There is far more that unites us than divides us . . . even on the subject of women's ordination.

- ▶ **Christ is the Head of the Church:** We all agree that Christ is the Head of the Church, and that it belongs to Christ alone (Eph. 1:22; Col. 2:10).

- ▶ **The Great Commission is for all:** We all agree that the Great Commission applies to every Christian, men, women, and children, and that the Spirit works through every believer around the world to accomplish that work.

- ▶ **Spiritual Gifts are Gender-Inclusive:** We all agree that every believer receives one or more spiritual gifts, so the gifts are gender-inclusive.

- ▶ **The Priesthood of All Believers:** We all agree that all Christians are part of the priesthood of all believers and have direct access to God through prayer, and that pastors and elders are not priests.

- ▶ **Full Equality by Creation:** We all agree that both men and women are fully equal because all human beings are created in the image of God.

- ▶ **Unity in Christ:** We all agree that in Christ "There is neither Jew nor Greek, there is neither slave nor free man, there is neither male nor female; for you are all one in Christ Jesus" and "heirs according to promise" (Gal. 3:28, 29).

▶ **The End-time Outpouring of God's Spirit:** We all believe in the end-time promise of Joel 2 in the Latter Rain: "I will pour out My Spirit on all mankind; and your sons and daughters will prophesy. . . . Even on the male and female servants I will pour out My Spirit in those days" (Joel 2:28, 29).

Position #1 *affirms all of these biblical teachings. It is not in conflict with any of them.*

In addition, the TOSC "Consensus Statement" shows that more than 90 percent of the committee agreed that the ordination of church leaders is biblical ("Study Committee Votes Consensus Statement on 'Theology of Ordination,'" *Adventist Review* [August 15, 2013], 8, emphasis supplied, also in all other quotations). We can only summarize a few points here:

1. Ordination is a biblical practice, setting apart ministers who oversee the church when they meet the scriptural qualifications.

2. The New Testament identifies two categories of ordained leaders:

   • Elders, including "supervising" elders who oversee multiple congregations); and

   • Deacons.

3. Some individuals are to be ordained for "global Church ministry."

The Main Question

There was only one question on which we had no consensus:

Do the biblical qualifications for the gospel minister who oversees the church allow a woman to be ordained to this office?

In answering this question, we should not overlook the fact that two of the three groups found clear evidence in Scripture for a iblical model of male leadership. Note this statement from "Position Summary #3":

> We believe that there is a biblical model of male ecclesiologi- cal *leadership* that has validity across time and culture.—*TOSC Report*, 100 (emphasis original).

So, even on women's ordination there is a clear biblical answer. It's found in 1 Timothy (see "Is 'Husband of One Wife' in 1 Timothy 3:2 Gender-Specific?").

Gender-Inclusive vs. Gender-Exclusive

Unlike most of Paul's letters, 1 Timothy is not written to a partic- ular church. Like Titus, it's written to a gospel minister. Its purpose is to give Timothy instructions on church order: "I write so that you will know how one ought to conduct himself in the household of God, which is the church of the living God, the pillar and support of the truth" (1 Tim. 3:15).

1. Gender-Inclusive (1 Tim. 2:1-7).

When Paul wants to be gender-inclusive, he uses gender-inclu- sive language, as he does repeatedly in 1 Timothy 2 (Gk. *pas, an- thrōpos*):

- ▸ Prayer should be offered for all people (vs. 1);

- ▸ God desires all people to be saved and come to a knowledge of the truth (vs. 4).

- ▸ Christ gave Himself as a ransom for all (vs. 6).

2. Gender-Specific (1 Tim. 2:8-15).

Paul also uses gender-specific language to explain how men and women should relate to each other in the worship setting.

Men

- ▸ Men are to take the lead in the church's worship and prayer (vs. 8).

Women

- ▸ Women should dress modestly

> ▶ They should not try to usurp the established teaching authority of the minister who oversees the church (vss. 912).

Paul bases this teaching on Genesis 2 and 3, which we'll come to in a moment: "For it was Adam who was first created, and then Eve. And it was not Adam who was deceived, but the woman being deceived, fell into transgression" (vss. 13, 14).

3. Gender-Exclusive (1 Tim. 3:1-12).

Beginning in chapter 3 with the qualifications for church officers, Paul uses even more specific, gender-exclusive language. He does not refer to just "anyone" but says, according to the NASB preferred by Position #2 (*TOSC Report*, 69, n. 9), "If any man aspires to the office of overseer, it is a fine work he desires to do" (vs. 1).

Then he lists the qualifications for this office:

"An overseer, then, must be above reproach, the husband of one wife. . . ." (vs. 2).

This is not just gender-specific, it's gender-exclusive, for several reasons:

> ▶ It is a fixed requirement, appearing three times: here and in Titus 1:6 for overseers/elders, and for deacons in 1 Tim. 3:12.

> ▶ Women assistants, sometimes called deaconesses, are referred to in vs. 11 as a group separate from both elders and deacons, with a different list of qualifications, so they cannot be included in either one.

> ▶ Paul uses the opposite phrase, "wife of one husband" in 1 Tim. 5:9, referring to widows. That means Paul meant what he said.

> ▶ If Paul had wanted to be gender-neutral, he could have combined these two phrases, "the overseer . . . must be the husband of one wife or the wife of one husband." But Paul didn't do this.

▶ Paul deals, in order, with smaller and smaller groups: first "all" (gender-inclusive), then "men" and "women" (gender-specific), and finally "husband of one wife" (gender-exclusive).

Note that the text says "must" (Gk. *dei*). The wording is as clear in Greek as it is in English. It's as clear as the command to "Remember the Sabbath day, to keep it holy" (Exod. 20:8).

Of course, this biblical command about ministers who oversee the Church is not one of the Ten Commandments, but it's still a command. The command to abstain from unclean foods is not one of the ten but it's still a command. So is Jesus' command to follow His example in washing each other's feet; and His command in connection with the Lord's Supper, "Do this in remembrance of Me" (1 Cor. 11:24) Or the Great Commission to, "Go, and make disciples . . ." (Matt. 28:19). None of these are part of the Ten Commandments, but they're still commands. They're not optional.

When Paul says "must," it's very clear. He even chose the strongest possible command form in Greek to say it.

The fact that Paul uses the Creation order from Eden as the basis for the roles of men and women in the Church shows two things: (1) this is a theological issue, not just a practical issue; and (2) these roles were God's ideal before the Fall and therefore reflect God's ideal for us today.

Studying the account of Creation and the Fall, we find that Paul and Genesis are in perfect harmony. They do not contradict each other.

Creation Order Leadership in Genesis

Genesis 1 describes the creation of the first human beings in these words: "God created man in His own image, in the image of God He created him; male and female He created them" (Gen 1:27.). Since both man and woman are created in God's image, both have equal value. Modern culture wants us to think that equal means identical. But equality does not destroy our uniqueness. Adam and Eve were alike in the ability to think and reason but different in temperament and body. They were also created by God at different times.

It is no secret why Adam was created first: because God gave him the primary leadership responsibility.

Order of Creation:

▶ Man – to keep the garden (Gen. 2:15)

   – told what to eat and what to avoid (Gen. 2:16, 17)

▶ Woman – given as man's "helper" (Gen. 2:18).

Manner of Creation:

▶ Eve shares with Adam the divine dominion (Gen. 1:26)

▶ He cannot lead without her because she is his helper (Gen. 2:18, 20).

In fact, the climax of this second part of the Creation account is not the creation of Eve but the creation of the family. Just as the Sabbath forms the climax of the first half of the Creation account (Gen. 2:1-3), God's marriage of the man and woman is the pinnacle of the second half (Gen. 2:24; cf. Matt. 19:4-6).

Genesis 3 relates the story of the Fall, and a reversal of the Creation order leadership principle.

Paul's reasoning in 1 Timothy 2 and 3 takes us back to this foundational leadership principle based on the Creation order: "Adam was formed first, then Eve" (vs. 13). By mentioning the Creation order, man first and then woman, Paul brings us back to Eden and shows that its ideal leadership arrangement is valid in the Church for all time.

Women Keeping Silent in Church

While 1 Timothy 3:2 is very clear—that the minister who oversees the Church "must be the husband of one wife," some say that if we're going to take this text literally, then, according to 1 Corinthians 14, women must keep silent in church.

Even with this passage, a plain reading of the text applies. Let's consider some important points about this passage:

▶ Unlike the Pastoral Epistles of Timothy and Titus, which were written to ministers serving many different areas, 1 Corinthians was written to a specific church in Corinth.

▶ It was written primarily to address specific issues and questions that came up in Corinth.

▶ 1 Corinthians 14 addresses the practices of three groups who were causing significant disruptions in the worship service at Corinth.

▶ These disruptions were caused by men as well as women:

❖ men were speaking in tongues without an interpreter (vss. 27, 28).

❖ men were prophesying without interpretation (vss. 29-33).

❖ women "kept asking questions" (Gk. *eperōtatōsan*) while people were speaking (vss. 34, 35).

▶ Paul commands all three groups to "keep silent"—using a very strong word in Greek (Gk. *sigaō*)—a word he doesn't use in 1 Timothy, where he instructs women during the worship service to learn quietly (1 Tim. 2:11, 12).

We need to remember Paul is not talking about a Sabbath School class but explaining how the Christians in Corinth can preserve reverence and decorum in worship.

Religious Offices in the OT and the NT

Let's return now to our main question: Can women also be ordained to serve as gospel ministers who oversee the Church?

To answer this question fully, we must look at what the entire Bible says—briefly because of time.

While we see a variety of female Bible characters who have important roles throughout Scripture (e.g., Miriam and Deborah in the Old Testament; Mary, Priscilla, Phoebe, Junia and others in the New Testament), two key points stand out:

- ▶ No woman was ever given a priestly role in the Old Testament.

- ▶ And no woman in the New Testament ever functioned as an apostle or gospel minister overseeing the Church.

Jesus, as the Head of God's Church in both the Old and New Testaments, has made very clear by precept and by practice who is to be ordained to this office.

1. Old Testament

In the Old Testament, even though Israel was a priesthood of believers (Exod. 19:5, 6), God commanded that *priests* and *Levites*—all men—be set apart to lead Israel in worship and religious instruction (Exod. 40:12-16; 29:9; Num. 8:10, 18-20; see Position #1, 21, 22). For both the priests and the Levites, clear qualifications and rituals were commanded for their ordination. These qualifications were not optional.

2. New Testament

In the New Testament Church, Jesus ordained twelve men as apostles. They were His gospel ministers to oversee the Church and were commissioned to ordain other leaders from every nation, kindred, tongue, and people (Matt. 28:19, 20; Rev. 14:6).

The gender requirements were not temporary. Even though Jesus and Paul emphasized that the gospel and even leadership was open to the Gentiles, the gender requirement was never changed. Paul refers to the Creation order to show its applicability for all time.

Paul and Barnabas "ordained elders in every church" and Paul likewise instructed Titus, "appoint elders in every city as I commanded you" (Titus 1:5).

In actual fact, gender is the fundamental qualification upon which the others are all built and "is a clear, unambiguous requirement that gives no room for misinterpretation or misunderstanding." (Position #1, 13, 14).

Some argue that if women can work in full-time ministry, why shouldn't we give them what some are asking for? Why not ordain them? We cannot do that for one simple reason:

It is not ours to give as we see fit, for God says that he (the minister) is to be "the husband of one wife" (1 Tim. 3:2) and that it is not permitted for a woman to usurp his authority as the gospel minister who oversees the Church (1 Tim. 2:11, 12). The Bible is so plain on this point in order that there would be no misunderstanding as to the qualifications for ordination to the office of gospel ministry.

The Jerusalem Council of Acts 15

Now let's briefly consider the Jerusalem Council as recorded in Acts 15. As you know, some Jewish Christians continued to believe in the temple, its services, and its laws, meaning, in their view, that Gentile believers, in order to be saved, had to be circumcised (Acts 15:1). Therefore, it was a theological issue that was at stake.

Circumcision was not instituted in the Garden of Eden like the Sabbath, the family, and Creation order leadership.

▸ Circumcision began with Abraham, who was the father of the Hebrews.

▸ Unlike the Sabbath and Creation order leadership, which cannot be changed, circumcision is connected with the ceremonial law (Acts 15:5).

▸ Like the ceremonial law, circumcision is a shadow pointing forward to the gift of the Spirit and the new birth symbolized by baptism.

❖ Peter indicates as much in his speech to the Jerusalem Council: God was "giving them [Gentiles] the Holy Spirit, just as He also did to us [Jews]; and He made no distinction between us and them, cleansing their hearts by faith" (Acts 15:8, 9).

❖ Like the ceremonial law, circumcision was a "shadow of things to come" and came to an end with the death of Christ and God's rending of the temple veil from top to bottom.

Creation Order Leadership	Circumcision
From Eden, like the Sabbath and the family	From Israel, like the ceremonial law
Began with Adam, father of human race	Began with Abraham, father of the Hebrews
Like the Sabbath, points back to Eden	Like the ceremonial law, points forward
Godly leadership	Foreshadowed baptism
Reality	Shadow
Unchangeable, for the church in all ages	Temporary, ended with death of Christ

The Jerusalem Council listened to all sides of the issue. However, because it was a theological matter, their decision was based exclusively on the Old Testament Scriptures and God's revelation given three times to Peter in vision.

The Jerusalem Council did not establish two different standards based on culture—one for Jewish believers and another for Gentiles. The decision of the council was a decision that pertained to all Christians everywhere—both Jewish and Gentile believers in Christ. And because of that, the result was a unified Church worldwide.

The Jerusalem Council did not institutionalize a division in the Church between Jews and Gentiles—just the opposite. They reaffirmed that Christ's death on the Cross broke down the wall between Jews and Gentiles: "For He Himself is our peace, who made both groups into one and broke down the barrier of the dividing wall, by abolishing in His flesh the enmity, which is the Law of commandments contained in ordinances, so that in Himself He might make the two into one new man, thus establishing peace" (Eph. 2:14, 15).

In other words, by its decision the Jerusalem Council declared that there was no such thing as Jew or Gentile anymore, and that all had to live by the same laws—the laws of the kingdom of heaven, as one people, united in Christ.

The Jerusalem Council shows us that when there is disagreement and dissension in the Church—we are not to look to our own culture for wisdom and guidance. Instead, God provides a solution based on Scripture and divine revelation.

Conclusion

1. Because *the issue we are facing today is theological* and connected with the Creation order, it is far greater than whether a woman should be ordained as a gospel minister overseeing the Church. The question is whether Scripture or culture will guide the Church.

2. As we have seen, Scripture, both Old and New Testaments, is clear, and if we compromise our faithfulness to Scripture on this point, we will have compromised our only basis of unity. As much as we appreciate diversity, *it is Scripture, our Bible-based faith and practice, that holds us together*, not diversity. It is this Bible-based unity that will protect us from the scourges of pluralism.

Our confidence in the unity of Scripture can only be maintained if we continue to interpret it in the way the Bible interprets itself. If we begin to interpret it differently in different places, there is nothing to keep the church from splintering over tithe, congregationalism, homosexuality, and other issues. Just as the Sabbath and marriage cannot be compromised without compromising the unity of the church, neither can the Creation order leadership given in Genesis and affirmed by Paul, because it applies to self-sacrificing leadership in the Church. That principle cannot be compromised without ultimately destroying the unity of the Church.

If we allow diversity here, it will divide us. It already *has* divided us to some extent. When Israel demanded a king, rejecting God's kingship and His plan for leadership over them, Israel was divided, and ultimately Israel was destroyed.

3. *The Jerusalem Council made its decision based on divine revelation.* After deep, thorough Bible study, we can reaffirm the scriptural basis for the decisions of the GC sessions in 1990 and 1995.

Position 1 respectfully and prayerfully recommends the following to the Seventh-day Adventist Church in its Way Forward Statement:

✓ Reaffirm and encourage, with public recognition and licensure, women whom God has called to gospel work;

✓ Provide enhanced access to educational opportunities for women in gospel work and ensure fair and just treatment upon their placement in ministry;

✓ Return to the biblical practice of electing and ordaining only men to the office of local elder throughout the world Church, while providing for women to serve as un-ordained Church leaders under certain circumstances;

✓ Retain the scriptural practice of ordaining/commissioning only qualified men to the office of pastor/minister throughout the world Church in harmony with the consistent example of Christ, the apostles, and the Adventist pioneers;

✓ Promote the greater development of various lines of ministry for women, according to their spiritual gifts, including but not limited to personal and public evangelism, teaching, preaching, ministering to families, counseling, medical missionary work, departmental leadership, etc.

Appendix 7

Why the Third Option Is Not an Option

By Pastor Jim Howard
Member of the General Conference Theology of Ordination
Study Committee
Personal Ministries Director and Evangelism Coordinator
Michigan Conference of Seventh-day Adventists
April 3, 2015

The third option in the discussion regarding women's ordination believes that male leadership in the home and church presents the biblical ideal, especially in light of critical passages in 1 Timothy, Titus, and 1 Corinthians. However, it argues that practical concerns (as prompted by diverse local situations) and a desire for unity may allow for women's ordination. We will now evaluate the claims that serve as the basis for this position.

Third Option Claim #1: Organizational or non-moral commands are open to adaptation.

The third option gives various biblical examples in an attempt to support the idea of adapting "divine ideals" when dealing with "non-moral" issues. The first was that of Israel's requesting and being given a king even though it was not God's ideal. The argument is that if God allowed Israel to stray from His ideal on a "non-moral" issue, then He will allow us to do the same by ordaining women to the gospel ministry.

The example of Israel requesting a king is hardly one that our church should emulate, as the results were disastrous—a permanent division in Israel, the destruction of the Northern Kingdom and the loss of ten tribes, widespread apostasy, etc. Furthermore, while God allowed ancient Israel to have a king contrary to His will, this does not give license to the present-day church to establish practices contrary to the teachings of Scripture. We must remember that Israel did not receive a king until *God Himself* allowed it in response to the prayer of Samuel the prophet (1 Sam. 8:7-9). God did not leave it up to the people. If in His wisdom, God allows a variation from His revealed will to teach the folly of such a course, this is His prerogative; it does not give permission to the church to deviate from biblical instruction.

In the end, such a decision would sadly resemble the system of the medieval church in which ecclesiastical councils have authority over Scripture, even the authority to modify divine instruction (see Dan. 7:25). While each of the third option's other biblical examples of "adaptation" could be disputed, the overarching problem is the same in each case—the conclusion that the church may adapt or disregard biblical instruction without clear direction from God through the Bible or prophetic guidance.

The third option argues that the office of elder/minister is adaptable because the specification of gender is merely a "functional, ecclesiastical norm." However, it offers no real basis for this assertion. Given Paul's emphatic language in 1 Timothy 2 and 3 ("I do not permit" and an overseer/elder "must be"), how do third option proponents conclude that the gender requirement for an elder or minister is nothing more than an ecclesiastical "norm"? And even if this claim could be proven, upon what grounds would this make the gender requirement open to adaptation? The third option offers no real answers to these questions from the Bible or the writings of Ellen G. White, leaving us to conclude that they are merely *assumptions.*

This is precisely where the danger of the third option lies. It fails to evaluate carefully the many examples of those who *assumed* that a "non-moral" command of God was flexible when it was not. Adam and Eve, Cain, Nadab and Abihu, and Uzzah were each punished for violating what appeared to be "non-moral" commands. Perhaps more relevant is the story of Korah and his friends, who were punished for an attempted adaptation to the "functional, ecclesiastical norm" of the priesthood (Num. 16).

The guidance given by the third option for when and how to adapt biblical instruction is both deficient and dangerous. Contrary to third option assertions, biblical commands do not fit so neatly into the separate categories of moral command or organizational ideal. What about tithing? The ordinances? Lifestyle teachings? Do we have the right to permit baptism by sprinkling, the use of leavened bread in communion, or the drinking of alcohol in moderation? Presuming to take upon ourselves the responsibility of calling biblical instruction flexible, when inspiration has given no such indication, is not only unwarranted; it is dangerous.

While recognizing the consistent pattern of male priests, apostles, and elders in the Bible, the third option fails to consider seriously that throughout all of salvation history no circumstance ever arose that would merit an exception to this pattern. Not a single clear example of a female priest, apostle or elder can be found in the Bible. Why would we assume that God would have us forsake this clear biblical teaching now, in the remnant church, just when Jesus is preparing a people for His coming?

Third Option Claim #2: Spiritual leadership necessitates ordination.

The third option contends, "The fact that nearly everyone agrees that women *can* carry a primary role of spiritual leadership *under certain circumstances* (e.g. as currently is happening in China) is significant."[1] However, there is an important distinction to be made here that the third option fails to recognize. When a father is absent from the home and the wife and mother must assume the primary position of spiritual leadership, this does not make her the father and priest of the home. Likewise, while it is true that certain circumstances may require women to carry "a primary role of spiritual leadership" in the church, it does not follow that they must also be ordained into the biblical office of elder/minister.

The example of China is not comparable since this area is not currently an organized territory of the church and cannot therefore be governed by official church policy. However, there are other areas of the world church where there are no qualified men, and where women serve admirably as unordained church "leaders" to provide management and leadership to local congregations. Ordained ministers periodically visit these churches to conduct ordinances and other official church functions. This arrangement adapts to local needs without sacrificing faithfulness to the biblical qualifications of the elder/minister. The third option, while rightly noting that circumstances may call for a woman to serve as a local church leader, fails to give any necessary reason for a woman to be ordained as an elder/minister.

Third Option Claim #3: The "gender qualification of elder" should not be held in a more absolute sense than the other qualifications.

It is true that we live in a less than ideal world. This causes us to elect elders who may not meet every ideal of the biblical qualifications. Some are less "temperate" than others, some are more or less "gentle," or "hospitable," etc. These qualifications are measured in degrees; and where degrees are involved, it is not safe for us to draw arbitrary lines. This is not so, however, with the gender requirement. Men are not more or less male. Gender is not measured in degrees. It is a clear, unambiguous condition of serving as an elder/minister that gives us no room for misunderstanding. Where prohibitions are measured in degrees, we must allow for the individual conscience and work of the Holy Spirit. However, where the prohibition is unambiguous we must draw the line in the same place that Scripture does. To do otherwise would be to disobey a clear command of God.

We should also remember that the elder's qualifications were presented within a larger context. They appear only a few verses after the Apostle Paul's prohibition in 1 Timothy 2:12, where he states, "I do not permit a woman to teach or to have authority over a man." The elder is the very one who must be "able to teach" (1 Tim 3:2) with the authority given by church appointment or election and publicly recognized by ordination. Therefore, the specification of the elder as male in chapter 3 ("husband of one wife" and "one who rules his own house well") is not just one of many flexible qualifications. Rather, the gender-exclusive language of chapter 3 is necessary in order to be in harmony with the prohibition of the Apostle Paul in chapter 2, that women are not to teach from the position of official church authority occupied by the elder/minister. There is no evidence of flexibility in Paul's language (not "I do not suggest," but "I do not permit"). And he bases this command not on culture or local circumstances but on the creation order and subsequent fall of Adam and Eve (see 1 Tim. 2:13, 14).

Third Option Claim #4: Every region of the church should be allowed to make its own decision regarding the ordination of women.

The decision made at the Jerusalem Council (Acts 15) is repeatedly used by both the pro-ordination and third option viewpoints to justify allowing each division or region of the church to choose for itself whether or not to ordain women. Referring to the final outcome on church issues such as women's ordination, the third option suggests, "The decision, though taken collectively, may not require uniformity of action on the part of all, as the Jerusalem council allowed Jews and Gentiles to approach circumcision and ritual differently."[2] This claim is categorically untrue. The Council's decision *did in fact require uniformity of action on the part of all.*

The key to understanding this fact is first to remember that the issue in Acts 15 was never whether or not Jews or Gentiles *could* be circumcised, but whether or not it was a *necessary requirement* for salvation (Acts 15:1, 5). And though many strongly believed that circumcision must be required of the believing Gentiles, the Jerusalem Council refused to honor their convictions. Furthermore, this decision applied to every believer everywhere and in every case. Absolutely no religious liberty, as defined by the third option, was given to those who wanted to require circumcision or teach that it was necessary for salvation. They were not permitted to do so, but were bound by the decision of the Jerusalem Council. Contrary to the third option's assertion, there actually was "uniformity of action on the part of all" the churches. Whether or not individual Jews or Gentiles could privately choose to be circumcised is a separate matter entirely and one that was never in question.

Using freedom of conscience to shape the church's beliefs and practices will open the way to the promotion of same-sex marriage, academic freedom for teachers of evolution in our schools, and other causes that may arise in the future. For many, these things are just as much a matter of conscience as is the ordination of women.

Third Option Claim #5: Its recommendation can preserve the unity of the church.

Though the third option expresses a concern for faithfulness to the Bible, one cannot escape the fact that its driving purpose is to preserve unity in the church. This, however, is a fundamental flaw. When unity is our primary concern, biblical faithfulness always suffers.

The third option appears to be making an effort to preserve or maintain unity where unity does not exist. The purpose of the worldwide study on ordination was to settle biblically what has been to the church an undeniable source of *disunity*. With this goal in view, the third option leaves us worse off than when we started. Rather than recommending a decision based upon the authority of Scripture, it attempts to eliminate the disunity by concluding that we are not bound to follow what the Scriptures teach on this particular issue.

Adopting the third option's recommendation would set a dangerous precedent. Instead of preserving unity, it would in effect institutionalize disunity and seriously weaken people's confidence in the Bible. Furthermore, it would threaten our identity as a truly worldwide church because it would move us toward a more congregational system of church governance, one in which each division, union, conference, and local church is free to do what is right in its own eyes (see Judg. 17:6; 21:25).

While claiming that disunity will result from our following God's will in this matter, the third option fails to consider the disastrous consequences of its own recommendation. Since it teaches that God's pattern and preference is to have male elders and ministers, dedicated church members may legitimately ask, "If we believe the Bible teaches that the elder/minister should be male, then why do we ordain women?" Pastors, evangelists, and other church leaders would be faced with the impossible task of explaining that with certain biblical instructions, if the duly authorized majority in a given sector of the church feels differently, we do not have to follow the Bible. Then, in our evangelistic outreach, appeals to follow the Bible rather than the precepts of men would sound hollow as we try to explain why, in certain cases, we as a church have chosen a different path from God's preferred will.

Ultimately, the third option sacrifices the persuasive power of our message and the mission of the church for the sake of protecting an imaginary unity. The end result would be to further strengthen the very thing it hopes to avoid. Not unity, but disunity, would be the sure result.

Conclusion

We have great sympathy for the third option's desire to hold together a church that is currently divided on the issue of women's ordination. However, its noble intent will never be realized by the plan it recommends. While it aims to preserve unity, it institutionalizes disunity. While it claims to leave our hermeneutics uncompromised, it introduces a foreign method of adapting biblical instruction that would be disastrous to our mission and even our credibility as a Bible-based church. While it seeks to protect gender distinction, it actually weakens it by calling the gender-specific language of the elder "only one among a number of qualifications." While it claims to prevent the mission of the church from being hindered, it in fact hinders the mission itself by implying to the unordained laity that ordination is necessary for *truly* advancing the work. And in an effort to protect religious liberty, it ends up marginalizing those whose consciences are bound by the clear teaching of Scripture.

When reading the third option's position summary, one may easily be influenced by the continual references to some biblical teachings as being *organizational* or *ecclesiastical*. These words have the effect of lessening the weight of the divine instruction, giving it a mere human quality and making it easier to view as flexible. We must remember, however, that the gender requirement of the office of the elder/minister is more than just an organizational guideline or ecclesiastical norm; it is a biblical requirement. This is not the *Church Manual* or working policy that we are dealing with here, but the Bible. We simply do not have the authority to adapt or disregard inspired instructions.

It is wishful thinking to believe that if the third option is voted then everything will be fine, our church can follow different practices in different places, and the mission will move forward. In reality, this first step away from scriptural practice is just the beginning. Should we would move away from our Bible base, we would open the door to many cultural pressures just waiting to have their say. As culture begins to displace Scripture in the decision-making process of some divisions, the pressure to conform will only grow. We must reaffirm and further develop the roles of women in ministry, but we must always remain faithful to God's Word.

Endnotes:

1. "Position Summary #3," p. 19, https://www.adventistarchives.org/position-summary-3.pdf (accessed April 3, 2015).

2. Ibid., p. 15.

Appendix 8

Summary of Theology of Ordination Study Committee Presentations: Looking at All Sides of the Issue

TOPICS	POSITION 1	POSITION 2	POSITION 3
Summary Position Papers	"Position Summary 1" (June 2014)	"Position Summary 2" (June 2014)	"Position Summary 3" (June 2014)
Way Forward Papers	"Way Forward Statement #1" (June 2014)	"Way Forward Statement #2" (June 2014)	"Way Forward Statement #3" (June 2014)
Evaluation of Positions	Evaluation of Position 1 by Position 2 Angel Manuel Rodriguez, "Evaluation of the Arguments Used by Those Opposing the Ordination of Women to the Ministry" (June 2014)	Evaluation of Position 2 by Position 1 Gerhard Pfandl with Daniel Bediako, Stephen Bohr, Laurel and Gerard Damsteegt, Jerry Moon, Paul Ratsara, Ed Reynolds, Ingo Sorke, and Clinton Wahlen, "Evaluation of Egalitarian Papers" (June 2014)	Evaluation of Position 3 By Position 1 "Women's Ordination: Group 1 Review of Position Summary #3" (Not Presented) *[End of Position 3 Papers]*
TOPICS	POSITION 1	POSITION 2	GENERAL PAPERS
Dealing With Church Controversies			Paul S. Ratsara and Richard M. Davidson, "Dealing With Doctrinal Issues in the Church—Proposal for Ground Rules" (January 2013) William Fagal, "The Proper Role of Ellen G. White's Writings in Resolving Church Controversies" (January 2013

To access the presentations in this Table, enter this link in your browser: https://www.adventistarchives.org. Table created by P. Gerard Damsteegt and William A. Fagal. Used by Permission. The columns have been adapted slightly for use here. Table continues on succeeding pages.

TOPICS	POSITION 1	POSITION 2	GENERAL PAPERS
History of Ordination			David Trim, "Ordination in Seventh-day Adventist History" (January 2013) Darius Jankiewicz, "The Problem of Ordination: Lessons from Early Christian History" (January 2013) P. Gerard Damsteegt, "Magisterial Reformers and Ordination" (January 2013)
History of Women's Ordination	Nicholas Miller, "The Ordination of Women in the American Church" (July 2013) P. Gerard Damsteegt, "Women's Status and Ordination as Elders or Bishops in the Early Church, Reformation and Post-Reformation Eras" (July 2013)	John W. Reeve, "Trajectories of Women's Ordination in History" (July 2013)	David Trim, "The Ordination of Women in Seventh-day Adventist Policy and Practice" (July 2013) Alberto R. Timm, "Seventh-day Adventists on Women's Ordination. A Brief Historical Overview" (Not Presented)
Theology of Ordination	P. Gerard Damsteegt, et al., "A Theology of Ordination: An Integration of Bible and Ellen G. White's Writings" (Not Presented)	Angel Rodriguez, et al., "Towards a Theology of Ordination" (January 2013)	
Ellen White on Biblical Hermeneutics			P. Gerard Damsteegt, "Ellen G. White on Biblical Hermeneutics" (January 2013)

TOPICS	POSITION 1	POSITION 2	GENERAL PAPERS
Biblical Hermeneutics	Edwin Reynolds, "Biblical Hermeneutics and Headship in First Corinthians" (July 2013) P. Gerard Damsteegt, "Hermeneutics: Interpreting Scripture on the Ordination of Women" (January 2014)	Jiri Moskala, "Back to Creation: Toward a Consistent Adventist Creation-Fall-Recreation Hermeneutic" (July 2013) Teresa Reeve, "1 Corinthians 11:2-16 and the Ordination of Women to Pastoral Ministry" (January 2014)	
Old Testament	Paul Ratsara and Daniel Bediako, "Man and Woman in Genesis 1-3: Ontological Equality and Role Differentiation" (July 2013) Laurel Damsteegt, "Women of the Old Testament: Women of Influence" (July 2013)	Richard M. Davidson, "Should Women Be Ordained as Pastors? Old Testament Considerations" (July 2013)	
New Testament	Stephen Bohr, "Issues Relating to the Ordination of Women with Special Emphasis on 1 Peter 2:9, 10 and Galatians 3:28" (July 2013)	Teresa Reeve, "Shall the Church Ordain Women as Pastors? Thoughts Toward an Integrated NT Perspective" (July 2013)	
1 Corinthians 11	Edwin Reynolds, "Biblical Hermeneutics and Headship in First Corinthians" (July 2013)	Teresa Reeve, "1 Corinthians 11:2-16 and the Ordination of Women to Pastoral Ministry" (January 2014)	
1 Timothy 2	Ingo Sorke, "Adam, Where are You?" (July 2013)	Carl Cosaert, "Paul, Women, and the Ephesian Church: An Examination of 1 Timothy 2:8-15" (July 2013)	

TOPICS	POSITION 1	POSITION 2	GENERAL PAPERS
1 Timothy 3	Clinton Wahlen, "Is 'Husband of One Wife" in 1 Timothy 3:2 Gender Specific?" (January 2014)	Carl Cosaert, "Leadership and Gender in the Ephesian Church: An Examination of 1 Timothy" (January 2014)	
Headship	John W. Peters, "Restoration of the Image of God: Headship and Submission" (January 2014)		
Ordination and Authority	Jerry Moon, "Ellen White, Ordination, and Authority" (July 2013)	Darius Jankiewicz, "Authority of the Christian Leader" (July 2013)	
Ellen White and Women's Ordination	P. Gerard Damsteegt, "Headship, Gender, and Ordination in the Writings of Ellen G. White" (July 2013)	Denis Fortin, "Ellen White, Women in Ministry and the Ordination of Women" (July 2013)	
Testimony	Phil Mills, "Church Unity, Testimony, and the Jerusalem Council" (June 2014)	Tara J. VinCross, "Our Testimony" (June 2014) Dwight Nelson, "My Personal Testimony: Some Pastoral Reflections" (January 2014)	